INSPIRING STORIES FOR CHILDREN

Volume 4

Bal-Mukund Character Building Series

Bal-Mukund Coordinator: Aruna Kannan
Editorial Team: Shreya Bhat, Anand Rao
Contributing Author: Anuradha Shankar
Illustrated by: Sanjay Sarkar
Design: Graphics Spot

Published by:
Jagadguru Kripalu Yog
7405 Stoney Point Drive
Plano, TX 75025
USA
www.jkyog.org

ISBN 978-0-9826675-3-8

Printed by:

Elegant Prints
www.elegant-prints.com

Dedication

The Bal-Mukund Character Building Series is dedicated to our Beloved Spiritual Master, Jagadguru Shree Kripaluji Maharaj, who is illuminating this world with the purest rays of Divine knowledge and love.

He has taught us by his example, the importance of nurturing children with love and care, to help them realize a glorious future. He has given us the supreme process of building a noble value system into impressionable young minds by teaching them selfless Divine love.

We pray that by his blessings this series will be helpful in inspiring, elevating and molding the children of today, who in turn will create a better world for tomorrow.

Jagadguru Shree Kripaluji Maharaj

पवित्र जीवन एवं महान व्यक्तित्व की नींव की प्राप्ति के हेतु बाल्यावस्था में ही दिये गये संस्कारों से पड़ती है। अतएव माता पिता का स बच्चों को सर्वश्रेष्ठ प्रेमोपहार यही होता है कि उन्हें बचपन से ही दैवी गुण सम्पन्न बनाया जाय।

उन दैवी गुणों का प्राकट्य परमात्मा की निष्काम भक्ति द्वारा अंतःकरण की शुद्धि से ही होता है।

अतः आध्यात्मिक शिक्षा द्वारा बच्चों के मन में भगवद् भक्ति का संचार करना उनके उज्वल भविष्य के हेतु सर्वाधिक कल्याणकारी है।

भक्त प्रहलाद ने कहा था –

कौमार आचरेत् प्राज्ञों धर्मान् भागवतानिह (भागवत ७/६/१)

अर्थात् बाल्यावस्था से ही भागवत धर्म का अनुसरण प्रारम्भ करना चाहिये।

यह 'बालमुकुन्द' चित्र निर्माण पुस्तक माला भारतीय संस्कृति एवं शास्त्रों के वेदों पर आधारित ऐसी ही कल्याण कारी आध्यात्मिक-शिक्षा युक्त है। मेरी शुभ कामना है कि बालवृन्द इस से अवश्य लाभान्वित होंगे।

अवदीम – जगद्गुरु कृपालु महाराज

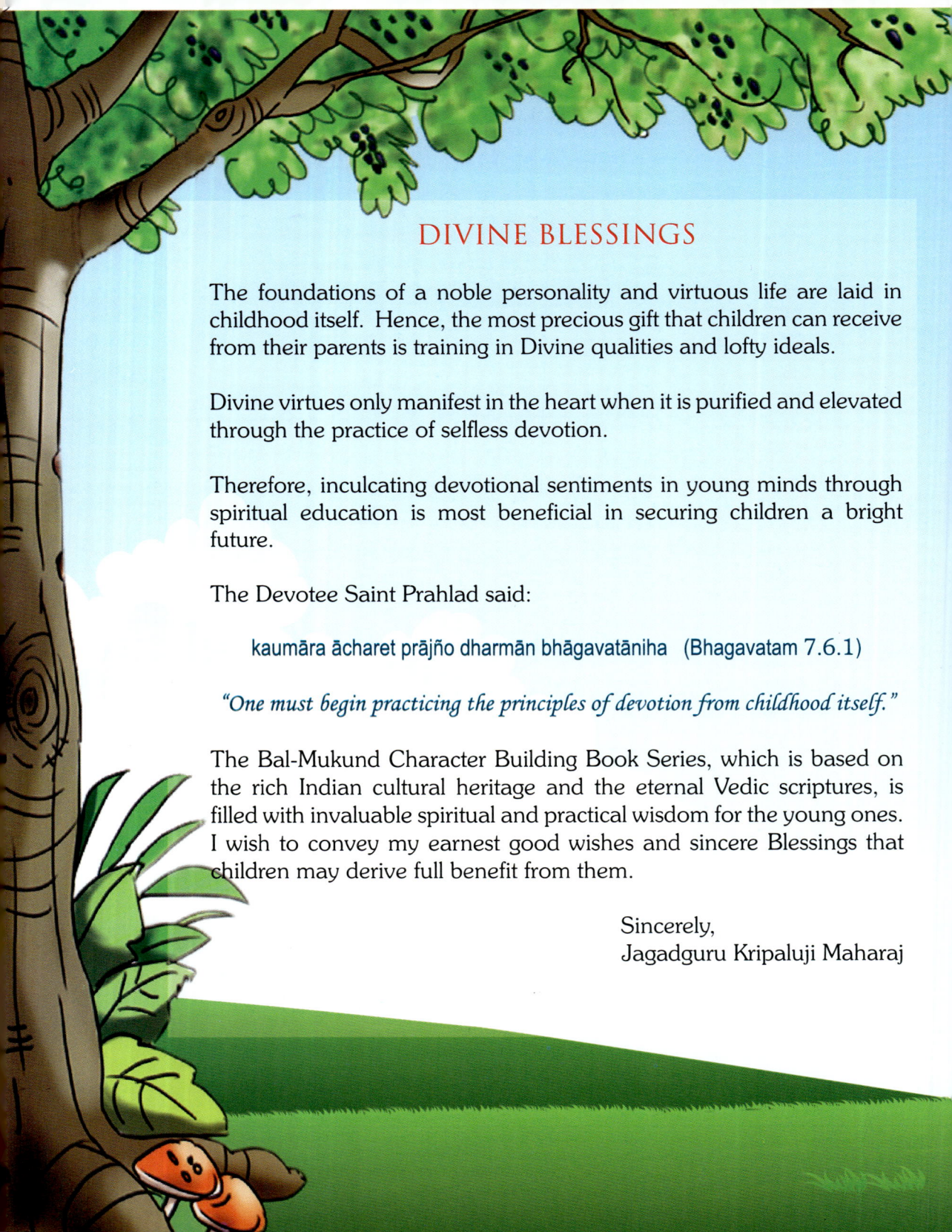

DIVINE BLESSINGS

The foundations of a noble personality and virtuous life are laid in childhood itself. Hence, the most precious gift that children can receive from their parents is training in Divine qualities and lofty ideals.

Divine virtues only manifest in the heart when it is purified and elevated through the practice of selfless devotion.

Therefore, inculcating devotional sentiments in young minds through spiritual education is most beneficial in securing children a bright future.

The Devotee Saint Prahlad said:

kaumāra ācharet prājño dharmān bhāgavatāniha   (Bhagavatam 7.6.1)

"One must begin practicing the principles of devotion from childhood itself."

The Bal-Mukund Character Building Book Series, which is based on the rich Indian cultural heritage and the eternal Vedic scriptures, is filled with invaluable spiritual and practical wisdom for the young ones. I wish to convey my earnest good wishes and sincere Blessings that children may derive full benefit from them.

Sincerely,
Jagadguru Kripaluji Maharaj

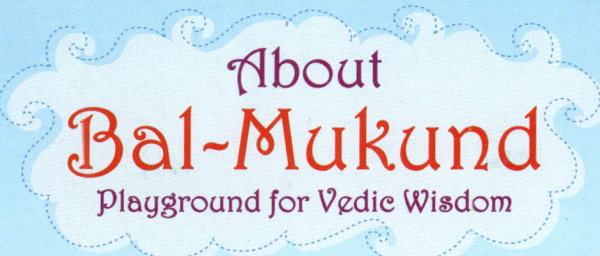

About
Bal-Mukund
Playground for Vedic Wisdom

Bal-Mukund is a specially designed personality development program for children, envisioned by Swami Mukundananda. It endeavors to:

❖ Educate young minds in the knowledge of Vedic wisdom to lead a virtuous life.

❖ Enthuse the spirit of giving with a service attitude.

❖ Encourage problem solving with courage, confidence and faith.

❖ Entertain creativity, expand power of concentration and focus.

❖ Elevate young minds to higher consciousness and fill their hearts with love and reverence for God.

The Bal-Mukund program is designed for the holistic development of a young one's physical, intellectual, social and spiritual faculties. Activities include Yoga, Pranayam, Meditation for children, Shlokas, Kirtans, Stories/discussion, Games, Language classes, Arts and Crafts.

For Bal-Mukund program details and centers:
www.bal-mukund.org

INTRODUCTION TO THE BAL-MUKUND CHARACTER BUILDING SERIES

The mark of a civilized society is the loving care it takes of its children. They are not merely children; they will soon be other people's husbands and wives, and parents of grandchildren. They possess God's life force that is yearning to make them Presidents, Scientists, Engineers, Doctors, Artists, Writers, and Musicians. Just as the acorn carries the potential of becoming an oak tree, children carry in them infinite potential for future greatness. Caring parents and teachers see this potential, and carefully cultivate and nurture it.

Parents and teachers are partners of God. They are working with the Creator of the Universe in shaping human nature and forging the future world. Each day they make deposits in the memory banks of their children. These deposits must be uplifting, and ennobling to their impressionable minds, which are sponge-like and very sensitive to the impressions they receive from their mentors. Children possess a remarkable amount of passion to go after their ideals. They throw themselves completely, heart and soul, into everything. The impressions they receive in these formative years mould their vision for the future. Loving parents and teachers teach their children to dream with their eyes open, of a noble and fulfilling life. They fill their hearts with lofty ideals and inspiring thoughts, and then fondly watch as their wards strive to attain the goals that have been mapped in them in their childhood.

Jagadguru Shree Kripaluji Maharaj teaches that best inheritance we can leave for children is good training in character building. A strong and sound value system built into them will remain until death. It will be the foundation for a successful and rewarding life. Hence, the values we inspire them to cherish are of paramount importance.

Children must be taught that money and luxurious possessions alone will not give happiness, but a virtuous life will be a continual feast.

Time spent in inculcating such values in children is an investment into the future. It is the finest gift of love from parents to their children. The Bal-Mukund Character Building Series contains invaluable instructions, famous verses, bhajans, stories, life histories and information about festivals, for building values in children. For ease of remembrance, the values that are required for triumph in life have been grouped with the letters of the acronym "KRIPALU". These set of values will teach children to be heroic from within, and instill nobleness in their thought, word and deed.

The compendium of stories, biographies, festivals, sayings, kirtans and prayers in this series of books has been chosen from the Vedic scriptures and the rich literary heritage of India. They convey powerful messages to educate, encourage, enthuse, and entertain young minds. Most importantly, they fill the heart with love and reverence for God, which is the essence of all morality. We hope they will be cherished by teachers, parents and children alike, who will meditate upon them, learn them and make them a part of their lives.

Swami Mukundananda

The "KRIPALU" Values

K for Kindness

Helping nature, Service attitude, Caring for others, Compassionate to the sufferings of others, Non-violence towards all beings, Forgiveness, and Seeing the Divinity in others.

R for Respect

Respect for Elders, Respect for Teachers, Respect for Authority, Respect for each other, Courtesy, Good Manners, Not seeing faults in others, Being non-judgmental, Acceptance of the differing viewpoints of others, Obedience to Elders and Authority

I for Integrity

Truthfulness, Purity of thoughts and intentions, Self-discipline and control over mind and senses, Restraint from temptation, Restraint from harmful influences like drugs, cigarettes, and alcohol, restraint from gambling, Associating with good people and giving up association of those who are a bad influence.

for Perseverance
Hardworking, Enduring, Patient, Dedication to the work at hand, Tenacity to bear difficulties and not give up, Overcoming obstacles through persistence, Keeping a positive "I can do it" attitude, Single-mindedness towards goal, Using tact and intelligence and mental power to solve a problem.

for Accountability
Taking full responsibility for ones deeds, Taking the onus for mistakes, Responsibility for correcting them, not blaming others or having a whining nature, Taking responsibility for organizing oneself and one's work, Accepting the law of karma that what happens to us is a result of our own actions, Being punctual to our time commitments.

for Love for God
Trust in God, Faith in His protection, Acceptance of His will, Keeping a positive attitude in every situation with Faith in His Grace, A Sense of Gratitude for all that God has given us, Belief that He is with us and watching us always, Doing all actions for His pleasure, unconditional devotion to Him.

for Unassuming
Modesty, Unpretentiousness, Simplicity, Humility, Not boasting or showing off, Reverence for the Greatness of God, Faith that everything belongs to God and not to us, Realizing that God has a grand scheme why things happen and we all have a tiny role to play in His design.

Contents

K for Kindness

The Kripalu value beginning with the letter "K" is Kindness.
The various aspects of kindness are:

- ❖ Helping nature
- ❖ Service attitude
- ❖ Caring for others
- ❖ Compassionate to the sufferings of others
- ❖ Non-violence towards all beings
- ❖ Forgiveness
- ❖ Seeing the Divinity in others.

Yudhishthir – The Righteous King

The great Mahabharata war fought between two factions of the same family – the Pandavas and the Kauravas – was an epic battle, fought by the righteous against the wrongdoers. It was a war that saddened everyone's hearts. Even as a last resort, war could only bring about destruction, and was to be avoided at all costs.

The Pandavas, under the guidance of Lord Krishna, won the great war, and ruled Hastinapur righteously for many years. Yudhishthir was a kind and just king who took care of his subjects as though they were his own children. He was good to all, no matter what their status or position. He not only cared well for his mother Kunti, but he also took good care of the old Dhritarashtra and Gandhari, the parents of his enemies the Kauravas, till the end of their lives.

One day, a messenger came to Hastinapur with the news that Lord Krishna had closed His manifest pastimes on earth, along with all his associates, the Yadavas. This news left Yudhishthir heartbroken and he felt the time had come for him to give up the throne and proceed to the forest. He could not bear to rule in separation from Shree Krishna.

When he put forth his intention of relinquishing the throne

and departing to the forests, his brothers and wife insisted on going with him. After handing over the reins of the kingdom to their grandson Parikshit, who was then a young boy, the Pandavas along with Draupadi left for the forest. Giving up all their wealth and weapons, clad like ascetics, they left on their last journey towards the Himalayas.

The people of Hastinapur were sorrowful to see their wise and noble king leave, and followed the Pandavas for a brief while before turning back. However, a dog continued to follow them towards the mountains. As they started ascending the mountains covered with snow, Yudhishthir turned to the dog, and asked it to return, explaining that it would be difficult to survive the extreme cold and rough terrain. The dog refused to turn back, and continued to follow Yudhishthir. One by one, Yudhishthir's brothers and Draupadi died on the way.

Finally, it was just

Yudhishthir and the dog who continued higher, towards the peak of the mightiest of the mountains. As they approached the peak, a divine being appeared with his chariot, and welcomed Yudhishthir, informing him that God had granted him a boon to attain His abode.

Yudhishthir replied, "O King, I am honored by your boon, but please tell me what has become of my brothers and my wife who departed this world before me." The divine being replied, "Do not worry about them. All your relatives have reached the abode of God, and are awaiting your arrival there, including Shree Krishna. Please climb into the chariot so that you can meet them soon." Yudhishthir was happy and moved towards the chariot, accompanied by the dog.

As the dog was about to step into the chariot, the divine being said, "Stop! Dogs are not allowed there." Yudhishthir was astonished as the dog turned its head and tail cast down. He said, "If the dog cannot ascend the chariot, neither will I. You may return without us. The divine being said, "But this is just a dog. You are a great king and a great human being, and you have earned the right to enter Golok, the abode of God. We cannot grant the same boon to a common dog."

Yudhishthir replied, "This dog followed me as I left behind all my personal possessions. He stayed with me even as my wife and my brothers departed for the divine abode. I cannot desert him at this stage, repaying his loyalty with ingratitude. I do not wish to enter the abode of God if he is not allowed to do so."

The divine personality continued to argue, pointing out that Yudhishthir had not even stopped to perform the last rites of his brothers and wife when they died along the way. Why should he now wait for a dog that was not even related to him? Yudhishthir patiently answered, "My brothers and wife completed their span of life on earth and passed on when their time came. We had

17

severed all bonds of family and relationships when we left our kingdom to enter the forest. Why should I stop for them when they have already gone on their way? This dog is in no way related to me, but it has given me company all along on this journey. It would be sheer ingratitude if I went on my way, abandoning him."

Seeing Yudhishthir adamant, the divine being thought for a while and said, "I cannot allow both of you to enter the abode of God together, but if you wish, you may exchange positions with him. He can go to Golok in your place, while you will enter hell in his place. Will you agree to this?" Yudhishthir replied, without even pausing to think, "I agree. Please take him to Golok in your chariot and I shall take his place in Hell." As Yudhishthir spoke these words, the dog disappeared, and Dharmraj, the lord of righteousness stood before him.

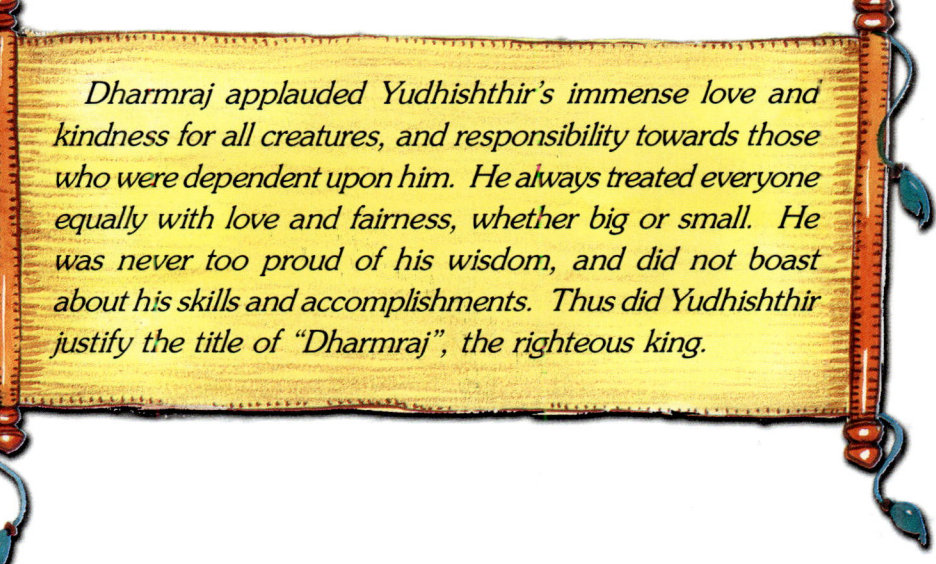

Dharmraj applauded Yudhishthir's immense love and kindness for all creatures, and responsibility towards those who were dependent upon him. He always treated everyone equally with love and fairness, whether big or small. He was never too proud of his wisdom, and did not boast about his skills and accomplishments. Thus did Yudhishthir justify the title of "Dharmraj", the righteous king.

Karna – The Generous

Of all the heroes from the Mahabharat, Karna stands tall for his generosity and his gratitude to those who aided him in his time of need. Although he was the son of Kunti, the mother of the Pandavas, he was fated to fight on the side of the Kauravas and against his own brothers.

Kunti was a young princess when the great sage Durvasa visited her father's kingdom. She took great care of the sage and looked to his comforts with humility. The sage was pleased and decided to grant her a boon. With his unique powers, he foresaw the future, and taught her a mantra that would invoke a celestial god of her choice, who would grant her a son.

The young Kunti was curious about the mantra, and seeing the sun shining brightly, invoked the Sun God, but was appalled when she found herself with a small child, bright as the sun itself, wearing golden earrings and armor. Afraid of the consequences of her rash action, Kunti abandoned the child, placing him in a basket to float down the river. The child was found by Adhirath, a charioteer of Hastinapur. Since Adhirath had no children of his own, he took the child as if he were a gift from God and brought him up as his own son.

Kunti was later married to Pandu, the king of Hastinapur, and had three children. Pandu had two more children through his second wife, Madri. These five children were known as the Pandavas. After the death of Pandu, it was Kunti who brought them up together, proud of her five sons, though never forgetting her first born, the one she could never call her own.

Karna grew up in the charioteer's house, but being from the lineage of warriors, he was naturally drawn to weaponry, and he tutored himself in the skills of warfare. Once, he mistakenly shot a cow and was cursed that he himself would be killed when he was as helpless as the cow he had slaughtered. In spite of such misfortunes, Karna continued to master all the skills that could be useful to warriors. He gained tutelage of the great Parshuram by concealing that he was a warrior, since Parshuram had a grudge against warriors and would never be willing to teach them.

One day, as Parashuram reclined on Karna's lap, am insect bit Karna, and, unwilling to wake the sage, Karna bore the pain as well as he could. The sage awoke and saw Karna's predicament, but was furious, for he realized that only a warrior could bear the kind of pain Karna had. He knew at once that Karna was a warrior and refused to accept Karna's assurance to the contrary. In his anger, the sage cursed Karna that since he had lied to his guru, he would forget the skill he had acquired when he needed it most.

Since he was considered to be the son of a charioteer, when Karna tried to prove himself as a talented archer, he was not allowed to display his skills against those of princes. Duryodhan recognized the talent of the

young man, and was quick to enlist his friendship, making him the King of Anga, thus elevating his status. It was a favor Karna never forgot, considering himself indebted to Duryodhan for the gesture. He stood by his friend through thick and thin, even after he learnt the story of his birth. While he was aware of Duryodhan's wrongdoing, and continually advised him against it, he was always grateful for his friendship, and always stood by his side, to the extent of fighting the war with Duryodhan even when he knew he was doomed to die.

Arjun and Karna were bitter enemies, especially since they were both equally adept at archery. Kunti worried about the rivalry between her sons and Karna. She recognized him as her abandoned son and regretted her hasty action. In an attempt to make amends, she went to meet him as he performed his oblations in the river, a ritual he performed every day at dawn. Surprised to see the mother of his rival waiting for him, he asked her the reason for her presence. Kunti related to Karna the story of his birth and begged him to join the Pandavas, his brothers. Karna was saddened by the tale, but he said, "I can never abandon Duryodhan, since he befriended me when I had no friends. I cannot be so ungrateful as to abandon him in his need." However, he reassured Kunti that his rivalry was with Arjun and Arjun alone. He would not fight or kill any of her other sons during the battle. He would only fight with Arjun.

Indra, the king of heaven, was also worried, since he knew that Karna was the only danger to Arjun. He also knew that as the son of Surya Dev, the Sun God, Karna was born with golden earrings and armor that made him invincible. He therefore decided to trick Karna into parting with them. Surya Dev was aware of Indra's intention, and warned Karna.

Indra arrived in the guise of a brahmin when Karna was completing his morning rituals, knowing that Karna would give

23

alms to the poor brahmins after he finished. Karna at once recognized Indra, but graciously asked him to accept something. Indra was waiting for Karna's word, and at once asked him for his earrings and armor. Karna smiled, and taking his knife, immediately cut off the armor that had grown with his body, and his earrings, and handed them over to Indra, remarking that he was happy to be able to give alms to the king of the heaven.

Indra was amazed by Karna's generosity, and offered him a boon in return. Karna asked for "Shakti", an invincible weapon that Indra possessed, which always found its mark. Indra had no choice but to grant his wish, but he added a condition that Karna would be able to use it just once.

Karna was surely one of the most generous of men, but his misfortunes in the form of various curses, and his bad choice of companions proved to be his downfall. Keeping his promise to Kunti, he refused to fight any of the Pandavas except Arjun, saving his most potent weapon for his archrival. Unfortunately, he was forced to use the weapon Shakti on Bheem's son Ghatotkach since nothing else seemed to work against the giant. At the final battle with Arjun, when his chariot wheel got stuck in the mud, he was killed while he was trying to get it out.

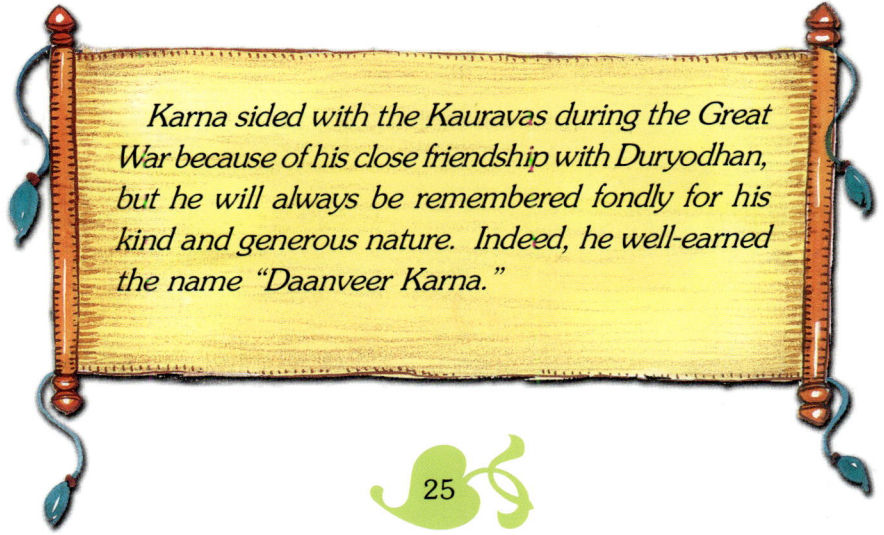

Karna sided with the Kauravas during the Great War because of his close friendship with Duryodhan, but he will always be remembered fondly for his kind and generous nature. Indeed, he well-earned the name "Daanveer Karna."

Lord Ram and the Squirrel

Lord Ram was not just a great king; he was the Supreme Lord Himself who had descended in the world. Yet, did you know that a little squirrel once helped Lord Ram? This is the story of how it happened.

The wicked demon king Ravan had carried away Seeta, the wife of Lord Ram, while he was in exile. Along with his brother Lakshman, Ram went in search of Seeta, and enlisted the help of the monkey king, Sugreev. Learning that Seeta was kept captive at Lanka, the kingdom of Ravan, which lay across the ocean, Ram along with the army of monkeys and bears arrived at the seashore.

To reach Lanka, they had to cross the vast ocean, and after much discussion, it was decided that a bridge would be built across the ocean. The multitudes of monkeys and bears that formed the army of Lord Ram were asked to bring stones and boulders to the seashore, so that a bridge could be built.

Shouting with excitement at the prospect of helping Lord Ram, the monkeys and bears ran around, looking for the biggest stones they could find. The monkeys were strong, and they carried huge boulders and even hills, on their shoulders easily, and dropped them in the ocean to help build the bridge.

26

The other animals at the seashore wished to help Lord Ram, and each of them helped in his own way. The fish and the other sea creatures did their bit by setting the boulders at the right place, while the birds flying overhead brought small stones to fill the gaps.

A tiny squirrel observed this huge effort, and he too wished to help. He thought for a moment, and then started collecting small pebbles lying on the shore, and dropping them in the ocean. After a while, he was too tired even to carry those pebbles, but still wanted to participate. He ran to the edge of the water, and, after rolling in the sand, ran to the water and washed himself. He ran back to the shore and rolled again, and more sand got stuck to him, since he was now wet. Again, he ran to the water to wash himself. The small grains of sand that stuck to his body were all he could contribute to the massive task of building a bridge across the ocean.

The monkeys laughed out aloud, and yelled, "Of what use are these tiny grains of sand, which can scarcely be seen among the huge boulders and hills we are bringing? Get out of the way and let us do our work!"

"Brothers, I too want to help you. These small grains of sand are all I can throw into the ocean as my contribution to the bridge. Please do not shout at me," said the tiny squirrel. The squirrel continued its work calmly. Finally, one of the monkeys, in his anger, picked up the squirrel and flung him far away from the shore.

Lord Ram, who was watching this, caught the squirrel before he fell, and set him down carefully. He then addressed His army, "O Vanars! You are brave and strong, and are doing a wonderful job lugging all these huge boulders and stones and dropping them in the ocean. However, did you notice that it is the tiny pebbles and stones brought by this tiny squirrel and other smaller creatures that are filling the small gaps left between the huge stones? Further, do you not realize that the tiny grains of sand brought by this squirrel are the ones that bind the whole structure and make it strong? Yet you scold this tiny creature and fling him away in anger!"

Hearing this, the Vanars were ashamed, and bowed down their heads in shame. Lord Ram continued, "Always remember, however small it may be, every task is important. A task can never be completed by the main people alone. They need the

support of all, and even though it may appear insignificant, an effort by any team member should always be appreciated!"

Lord Ram then turned to the squirrel and said softly, "My dear squirrel, I am sorry for the hurt caused to you by my army, and thank you for the help you have rendered to me. Please go and continue your work happily." Saying this, He gently stroked the back of the squirrel with His fingers, and three lines appeared where the Lord's fingers had touched it.

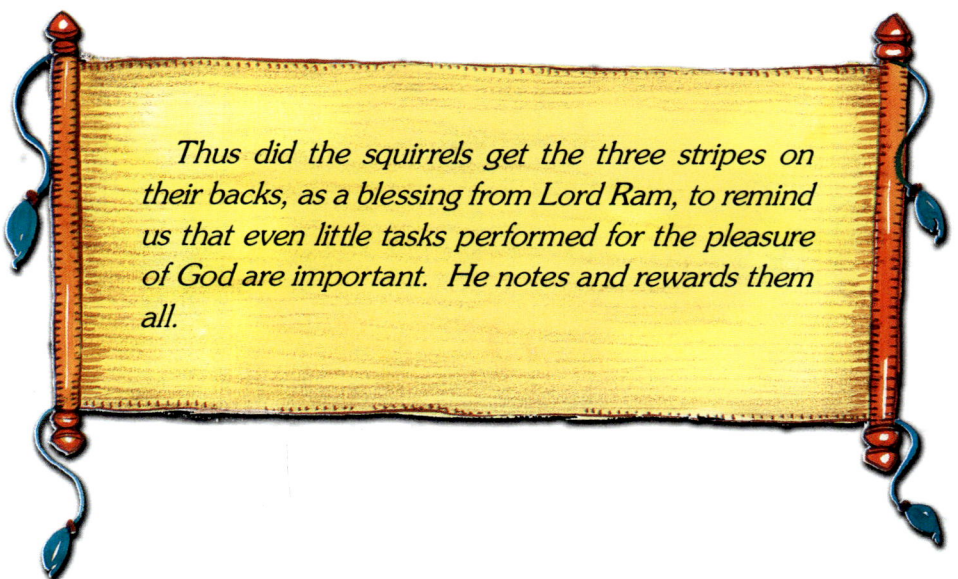

Thus did the squirrels get the three stripes on their backs, as a blessing from Lord Ram, to remind us that even little tasks performed for the pleasure of God are important. He notes and rewards them all.

The Noble Stag

King Brahmadutta of Kashi was fond of hunting. He made frequent hunting trips to a huge forest on the outskirts of the city, that was filled with deer and a mighty stag.

Once during the hunt, he warned his courtiers not to allow a single deer to escape or he would severely punish them. Forming a tight circle, they decided to drive all the deer in the direction where the king stood waiting. The courtiers surrounded the thicket and beat their sticks on the ground to drive out the deer. They saw a huge stag run out of the bushes. Since their circle was so tight, the only escape route that the stag could see was towards the king, who stood alone in that direction.

The stag looked him straight in the eye and sprinted towards him. Surprised, the king shot an arrow at the deer, but missed the mark. When the stag rolled over, the king assumed that his arrow had found its mark. Suddenly the stag jumped up and shot passed the kings men. When they realized that the king had missed him, they started to snicker at him.

The king always thought of he was an excellent marksman, and could not bear the taunts of his men. He set off into the forest in order to catch the stag. He chased the stag for quite a while and covered a long distance.

The stag came upon a hole in the ground that was covered by a rotting tree and filled with slime. From a distance, it could smell the dirty water and so was careful not to run over it. However, the king could not smell the pit and fell right into it. The stag realized that he was not being followed any more, and guessed that the king may have fallen into the pit.

When he went back to the pit, the king was struggling for his life. Feeling sorry for him, the stag decided to save his life even though the king had chased him with the intention of killing him. He told the king not to worry and to be brave. He held a huge rock with his hind legs and lowered himself into the pit. The king held on to the stag's neck, and the stag climbed out onto the level ground and carried the king to safety.

Thanking the noble stag the king asked him to return with him to Kashi, where he could

live with him. The stag had no interest in staying in a palace, and turned down the offer of the king. He requested the king to return and rule his kingdom wisely, with kindness and compassion. Saying this, the noble stag disappeared into the forest.

With a heart filled with humility and gratitude, the king returned to Kashi and proclaimed that all his subjects were to live a life of goodness, kindness and generosity. That night he went to bed a changed man and woke up singing praises of the stag. The head priest of the palace heard the king chanting a hymn in praise of the stag. He entered the king's chamber and remarked that on the previous day the king had been saved by a stag. The king was surprised and asked the priest if he could read minds. The priest answered that the hymn he sang in praise of the stag had described all the events.

The king resolved to live a virtuous and generous life. He vowed to give alms regularly to the poor. All his subjects also followed the example set by their king, and the city of Kashi witnessed a golden period.

Such good deeds took many souls to heaven. Indra, the king of heaven began to wonder where all these new sons and daughters were coming from. He then recalled the incident when king Brahmadutta's life was transformed by the stag and realized that the subjects of the king too had been transformed. That explained the large number of righteous souls in heaven. Indra now deciding to test the goodness of the king, made himself invisible and came down to earth.

On that very morning, the king was in the royal park with his priest and was doing his routine target practice. Just as the king was about to shoot the target, Indra made a stag appear before the target. The king immediately put his bow and arrow down. Indra spoke through the priest and encouraged the king to shoot the stag saying that his meat was very tasty and fit for a king.

The virtuous king refused to kill the stag saying that his life had once been saved by a stag, and he would not perform such a dastardly deed. The priest continued to tempt him and said, "If you kill the stag, you shall be made the king of gods. If you fail, you will be sent to hell along with all your children and the queen." But the virtuous king chose hell and sure death over hurting the beloved friend who had saved his life. Impressed, Indra appeared in his real form to greet the king. Blessing the king to have a long and fruitful reign on earth, Indra returned to his heavenly abode.

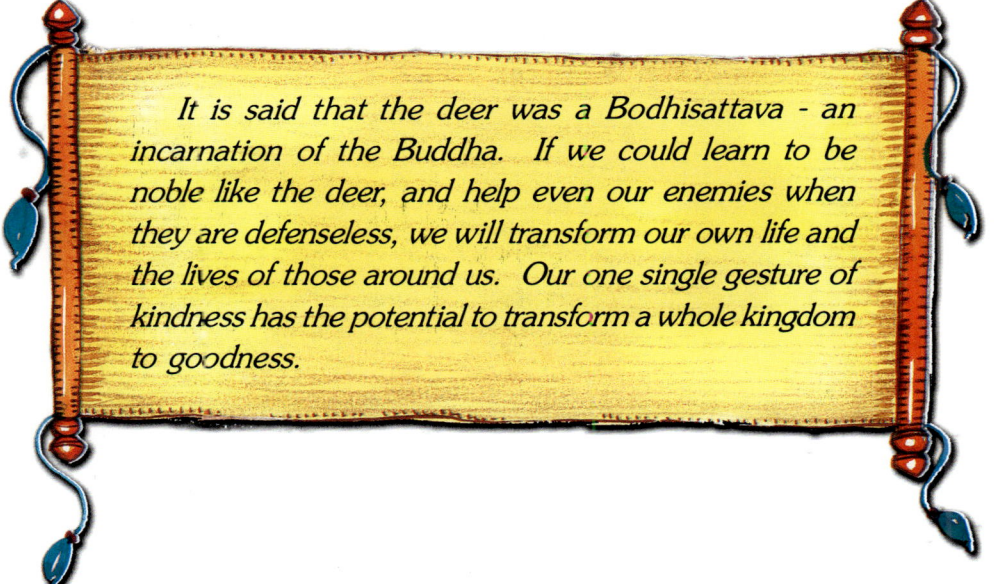

It is said that the deer was a Bodhisattava - an incarnation of the Buddha. If we could learn to be noble like the deer, and help even our enemies when they are defenseless, we will transform our own life and the lives of those around us. Our one single gesture of kindness has the potential to transform a whole kingdom to goodness.

R for Respect

The Kripalu Value beginning with the letter "R" is Respect. The various aspects of respect are:

- ❖ Respect for Elders
- ❖ Respect for Teachers
- ❖ Respect for Authority
- ❖ Respect for each other
- ❖ Courtesy
- ❖ Good Manners
- ❖ Not seeing faults in others
- ❖ Being non-judgmental
- ❖ Acceptance of the differing viewpoints of others
- ❖ Obedience to Elders and Authority

Uddalak

In the ancient days, students traveled long distances to seek a Guru who would impart them knowledge. The disciple had to live in the *gurukul*, the residential school of the Guru, along with other students, and serve the Guru with devotion in order to receive the knowledge.

Aruni of Panchal in Northern India was a dedicated student of the sage Ayodhaumya. Many bright disciples studied under the same Guru along with Aruni, who was not a bright student, but had staunch faith in his Guru. Many of the young disciples who were studying the Vedic scriptures ridiculed and humiliated Aruni for his lack of scholarly skills or aptitude to learn the sacred texts. Yet, he performed his duties diligently under the guidance of his master.

It was a cold winter evening and Aruni was carrying firewood he had collected for use in the ashram. Disciples did not carry any protective clothing in the winter, except for the ashram attire. The *gurukul* also had a garden, an orchard and large paddy fields. It was the duty of the disciples to till the fields and tend to the orchards daily.

On his way back to the ashram, it started to rain heavily while Aruni was walking through one of large paddy fields. Suddenly, he found a breach in the mud embankment that held back the water used to feed the paddy saplings. He realized that the water would wash away the mud bank, and the crops would die with no water.

Aruni wondered, "What can I do? If I stop to build an embankment, I will not be able to reach the ashram on time, and there will be no firewood at the hermitage to keep the place warm. I must hasten to the ashram with the firewood and rush back to the fields to plug the breach."

Meanwhile at the *gurkul*, sage Ayodhaumya and his disciples had assembled for the day's lessons. Drenched and shivering, Aruni rushed in, dropped the firewood in the courtyard, and told his teacher about the breach in the paddy field. Sage Ayodhaumya instructed him to take care of the breach and come back to the ashram after ensuring that the water does not escape. Paying obeisance to his master, Aruni ran back to the affected spot.

Not worried about the pouring rain, he set out to stop the leakage of water using logs and mud. However, this did not stop the leak. The heavy pressure of water washed away the temporary dam that Aruni made. He tried again but without much success. He felt helpless and it seemed impossible for him to stop the leakage. He reminded himself of his master's orders and that he must carry out his master's wishes at any cost.

Left without a choice, Aruni decided to plug the large breach by laying himself flat on the ground and creating a dam with his own body. The ice-cold water splashed against his back but Aruni did not budge. He stayed put to ensure the water did not flow away.

Night descended over the *gurkul* and the students retired to their living quarters to wind up for the day. Nobody ever thought or remembered where Aruni was. Soon, the ashram fell asleep

and the lights were out. The rain lashed all night but Aruni did not move from his position. He was determined to fulfill the wishes of his master by stemming the flow of water, thereby ensuring enough water for the fields. He knew that if he let go his position, the dam would burst and water would gush out. Aruni lay still in the freezing water all night long.

At daybreak, the teacher called out for Aruni but he did not get an answer. He asked his other disciples to look for him but they could not find Aruni. Sage Ayodhaumya was now worried for his pupil. Suddenly, one of the students realized that Aruni had gone to the fields last evening and never returned.

The Guru called his disciples and set out looking for Aruni. They reached the paddy fields and started to call out Aruni's name loudly. As he called out, he heard a faint voice, "Here I am Gurudev. If you say, I will get up, but the water will flow away."

The teacher and his disciples rushed to the spot and saw Aruni

lying on the breach, in order to hold the water back in the field. The disciples quickly pulled Aruni out from the freezing water. Sage Ayodhaumya was overjoyed to see his pupil carry out the instructions given to him with such unswerving dedication and sincerity. Filled with joy for his disciple, the sage asked Aruni to get up. He embraced Aruni and blessed him saying, "You shall be known as one of the greatest disciples in this world. Since you placed yourself at the breach to save the water, you will be called *Uddalak*, or one who arose from a dam. I grace you with the knowledge and wisdom of all the scriptures."

The sage continued to bless his disciple, "You shall forever be renowned for your unmatched devotion and obedience to your Guru." Aruni went on to become the famous sage Uddalak, whose teachings are a part of the Upanishads.

Uddalak demonstrated unwavering faith in his Guru's instructions. His only aim was to fulfill his master's desire by obeying him, and offering his own life in order to honor his Guru's words. Complete belief in the Guru's words, and the determination to uphold a Guru's orders are the hallmark traits of a true disciple. Although his fellow classmates were more learned and intelligent, they could not match Aruni's faith in his Guru. This unflinching faith made him finally surpass everyone in scriptural knowledge, with the grace of his Guru.

Puru – The Obedient Son

Yayati, the son of Nahush, was an ancestor of the Pandavas. He was married to Devayani, the daughter of Shukracharya, the guru of the asuras. However, Sharmishtha, the daughter of the *asura* (demon) king *Vrishaparva*, and a rival of *Devayani*, also fell in love with him, and they secretly got married. Yayati had two sons from Devayani – Yadu and Turvasu – and three sons from Sharmishtha – Druhyu, Anu and Puru.

One day, Devayani discovered her husband's secret marriage with her archrival, and was furious. She rushed to her father, complaining about it. Shukracharya was a powerful sage who loved his daughter very much. Saddened by her predicament and angry with his son-in-law, Shukracharya cursed Yayati saying he would lose the youth and strength of which he was so proud. Immediately, Yayati grew prematurely old.

Stricken with old age in his prime of youth, Yayati begged for forgiveness, reminding the sage that he had once rescued Devayani from a well. The sage relented and told him that while the curse could not be revoked, he could exchange his old age with anyone who would agree to give him his youth in return.

While Yayati had grown prematurely old, his desires had not abated, and he found himself with the cravings of youth in the body of an old man. Eager to revert to his normal appearance, he returned to his kingdom, trying to find someone to exchange his age with. However, he was unable to find anyone who would agree to such a deal, and he turned homewards, hoping that one of his five young sons would help him out.

He went to his oldest son, Yadu, and asked him to exchange his youth with Yayati's old age, but Yadu flatly refused. "People will laugh if they see me so old. You have four more sons whom you love more dearly than me. Why don't you go and ask them?" Next, Yayati went to Turvasu, who said, "Father, please excuse me. I do not want to grow old so soon. Ask one of your other sons."

Yayati went to Sharmishtha's sons, since it was his marriage to Sharmishtha that had resulted in his premature aging. Druhyu refused him, and said, "Father, if I take your age, I will be unable to do any of the activities I enjoy. I cannot agree." Anu, the fifth son was no more helpful, and said, "The aged are helpless and cannot do anything by themselves. I am too young to accept this, so father, please forgive me."

Yayati was devastated by the refusal of his four sons. His last resort was his youngest son Puru. If Puru refused, he would have to stay an old man for the rest of his life. He went to Puru and asked, "You are my youngest and dearest son. I have been afflicted by old age due to the curse of Shukracharya. If you take this old age for a few years, and give me your youth, I will enjoy life for a little longer. I promise to return your youth when I satisfy my desires. All your four brothers have refused, and you are my only hope. If you do not agree, I shall be stuck like this for the rest of my life, however long it might be."

Upon seeing the piteous state of his father, Puru was moved, and said, "Father, you have given me life. To give you my youth is the least I can do for you." Saying this, he embraced his father. As soon as the father and son touched each other, Puru assumed the old age of his father while Yayati became as youthful as his youngest son.

Leaving the aged Puru to rule the kingdom in his place, Yayati roamed the three worlds, experiencing sensual pleasures and hoping to fulfill his cravings. Puru proved himself a just and able king and gained great renown, while Yayati wandered around in search of elusive sensory happiness.

After years of such aimless wanderings and indulgence, Yayati realized that giving in to his desires served no purpose. They would subside for a moment and then come back with redoubled intensity. It was like attempting to quench a fire by pouring *-ghee,*

or clarified butter on it. Returning to his kingdom, he approached King Puru and pleaded him to take back his youth he had so kindly given him, and return the old age.

From the wisdom gained through his bitter experience, he advised Puru, "My son, freedom from desires is the only way to gain true happiness." Giving up his kingdom to Puru, he decided to go to the forest to perform penance. Yayati's decision of giving the kingdom to Puru was questioned by many, since he had four older sons, and according to tradition, it is the eldest son who inherits the kingdom. When he was asked the reason for this decision, he said, "When a father asks for something from a son, it is not to be taken as a request, but a command. When I asked my elder sons for their youth, they flatly refused, thus disrespecting and disobeying me. A son who disobeys his father is not a worthy son. It was my youngest son, Puru, who truly loved and respected me, and obeyed my wishes. Thus, he alone is my true son, and it is he who deserves to rule my kingdom."

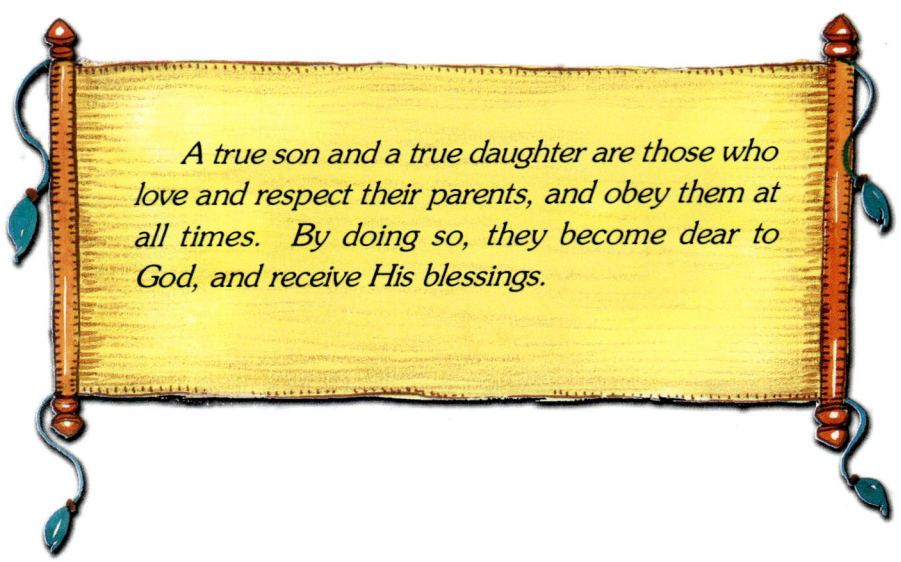

A true son and a true daughter are those who love and respect their parents, and obey them at all times. By doing so, they become dear to God, and receive His blessings.

Bheeshma

Shantanu, the king of Hastinapur married Ganga, the goddess of the holy river, and had a child named Devavrat. After the child was born, Ganga left the palace of Shantanu, to reside in her holy abode. The little Devavrat spent his early years with his mother, being taught by the gods and the greatest of the rishis, and returned to his father as a young boy.

Shantanu was so happy to see his son back that he anointed him as the crown prince.

Shantanu had lived an austere life since the departure of Ganga. However, one day, as he walked along the banks of the river Yamuna, he smelled a wonderful fragrance, and probing, he traced the fragrance to a young fisherwoman. He was surprised that such a divine fragrance could emanate from a common fisherwoman, and asked her who she was.

"I am Satyavati, the daughter of the chief of fishermen" she said, and added that the fragrance emanating from her was the gift of a sage she had pleased. Shantanu was so enamored by her that he asked her to marry him, but she replied that it was up to her father to decide whom she would marry.

Shantanu sought out the chief of the fishermen, and humbly requested his daughter's hand in marriage. Satyavati's father replied, "O King, we are flattered and honored by your request. We know you are a great king, and we respect you. It would indeed be an honor for my daughter to become your queen. However, as chief of my clan, I have a condition to put forward. The son born to you from my daughter should be king after you. If you agree to this, the marriage can take place at once."

Shantanu was stunned. He had already anointed Devavrat as his heir-apparent. Moreover, as his first-born child, and an able one at that, Devavrat certainly had every right to the throne. How could he now promise the fisherman that his grandson alone would be king? It would be unfair, and above all, Shantanu was known as an impartial and just king. This could not happen.

Shantanu sadly returned to the palace, knowing that though he had lost his heart to Satyavati, he would never be able to marry her. Devavrat soon became aware that something was troubling his father, even though he tried to conceal his sadness. When a

straight question failed to bring forth a clear answer, Devavrat questioned the charioteer about the places his father had recently visited, and soon arrived at the fisherman's doorstep.

Learning that his father had been enamored by Satyavati, he asked for her hand on behalf of his father. Satyavati's father replied, "O Prince, your father did come here and ask for my daughter's hand, but he could not meet the condition I set for him. As a king, I can understand his predicament, but as a father, it is my duty to ensure a bright future for my daughter and her children. My condition still stands. If your father agrees to it, I will consent to the marriage."

Devavrat asked, "Sir, please let me know the condition you have set for your daughter's marriage. I will fulfill it on behalf of my father." The chief explained, "Prince, if my daughter is to be the queen, I desire that it should be her children who should rule Hastinapur after the demise of your father. The king has already named you as his successor, and hence cannot agree to this condition."

At once, Devavrat replied, "If that is all, I pledge that it shall be the son born to your daughter who shall be the king. I renounce my right as heir to the throne." However, the fisherman was not satisfied, "Prince, you are a man of your word, and I believe you when you say that you will lay no claim to the throne, but what of your descendants? They will surely be as heroic as you, and will be serious contenders to the throne. How can you assure my daughter's children their rights?"

Devavrat was determined to fulfill his father's desire, and scarcely waited a moment before raising his right hand to the heavens and declaring, "I vow that I shall never marry and beget children. I shall remain a bachelor and dedicate my life to the throne of Hastinapur."

As he uttered these words, flowers rained from the heavens, and the skies resounded with cries of "Bheeshma! Bheeshma!" *Bheeshma* means the one who undertakes a terrible vow, and fulfills it. From then on, Devavrat came to be known by the epithet *Bheeshma*.

Satyavati's father was satisfied by the terrible vow of the young prince, and he allowed him to lead his daughter to marry the king. When Shantanu heard of the great oath taken by his son, he was overwhelmed with love and blessed him. He conferred upon him the gift of *iccha mrityu,* or the ability to choose his time of death.

Bheeshma observed his oath till the end of his life, ably justifying his name. He remained true to Hastinapur, guiding the sons and grandsons of Satyavati in their duties. He was always aware of the righteousness of the Pandavas, and encouraged them on their adherence to truth. Well aware of the wrongdoings of the Kauravas, he continually advised Dhritarashtra to be stern with his sons, especially Duryodhan. Even when he realized that his

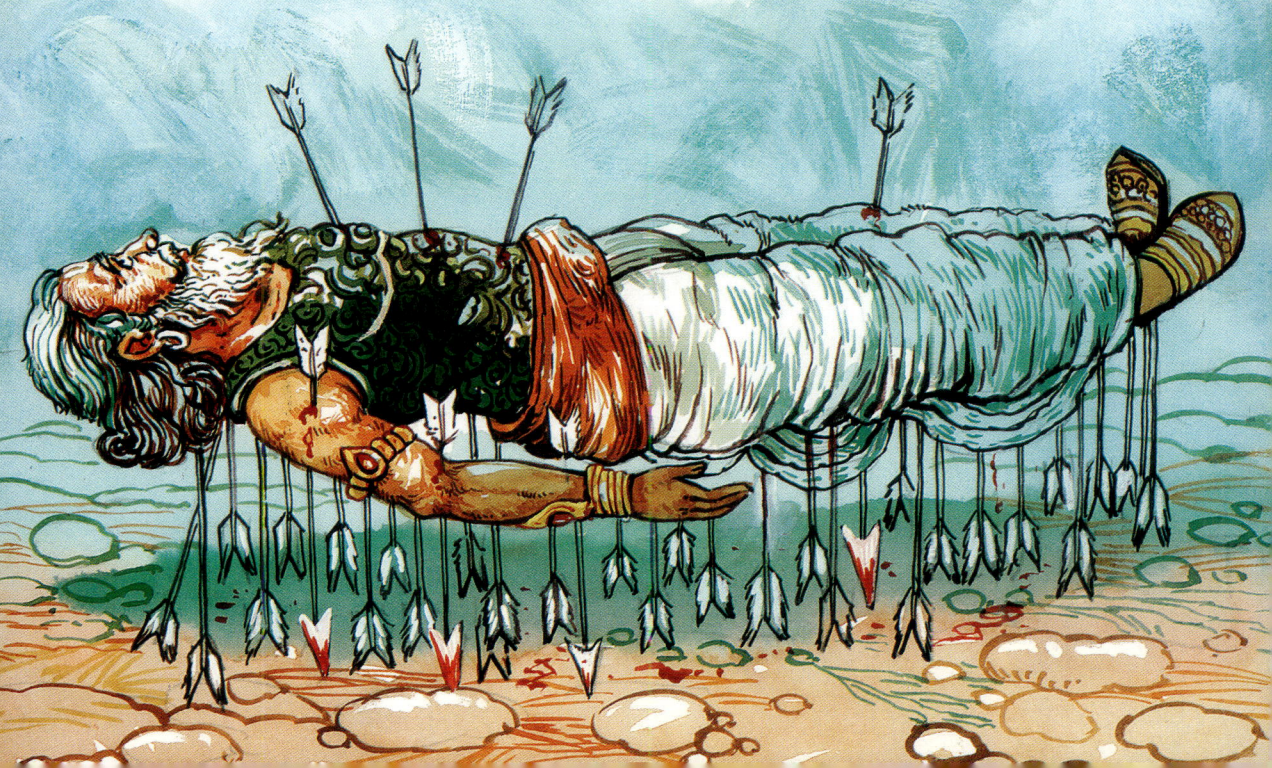

advice fell on deaf ears, he nevertheless continued to advise the king, as a duty towards the throne of Hastinapur. He was among the few people who realized the Divinity of Shree Krishna, of whom he was a great devotee.

During the war of Mahabharat, Bheeshma decided to stand by his oath towards the kingdom, and sided with the Kauravas, even though he knew the outcome of the war. His chivalry did not leave his side even in his last moments, when he refused to fight Shikhandi, aware that he was really a woman born to destroy him.

Lying on a bed of arrows, life ebbing out, he refused to leave the body and chose to cling on to life till the war was over and Yudhishthir was crowned the king, so that he could instruct the righteous king about his duties. It was only after he finished his discourse to Yudhishthir that he welcomed death with open arms, having completed all the vows he had taken upon himself.

The story of Bheeshma illustrates the importance of not compromising on our principles. Out of respect for his father, Bheeshma took an oath that he would always act in the best interest of Hasthinapur. He stayed true to his oath and lived his life to fulfill it. He had to make many sacrifices and uncomfortable choices along the way, but he never wavered.

I for Integrity

The Kripalu value beginning with the letter "I" is Integrity. The various aspects of integrity are:

- ❖ Truthfulness
- ❖ Purity of thoughts and intentions
- ❖ Self-discipline and control over mind and senses
- ❖ Restraint from temptation
- ❖ Restraint from harmful influences like drugs, cigarettes, and alcohol
- ❖ Restraint from gambling
- ❖ Associating with good people
- ❖ Giving up association of those who are a bad influence.

Harishchandra – The Truthful King

Harishchandra, the son of Trishanku, was an ancestor of Lord Ram. He ruled over Ayodhya with his wife and son Rohitashwa. He was a just and kind king. All his subjects led a happy and peaceful life during his reign.

Harishchandra had appreciated the value of truthfulness from childhood, and had vowed never to tell a lie, or go back on his word. In time, he gained fame for his honesty, truthfulness and integrity. This fame reached the ears of the celestial gods in heaven, and they decided to test him.

Sage Vishwamitra was selected for the task. Scheming to test the king, he tried in many ways to get Harishchandra to lie or to break a promise, but his efforts were in vain. Harishchandra was as committed to his values as the celestial gods had heard.

Finally, Vishwamitra came to Harishchandra in a dream and made him promise to give him his kingdom. He then reminded Harishchandra of the dream and asked him to fulfill the promise he had made in it. Harishchandra sacrificed his kingdom and everything he possessed to the sage, to begin a new life as a commoner with his wife and son. Amazed by such generosity, and increasing the severity of the test, Vishwamitra asked him for *dakshina,* the donation which is given after charity.

The king, having given up everything he owned, had nothing left to offer as *dakshina.* At the same time, he was unwilling to commit the sin of refusing to give *dakshina.* Asking Vishwamitra for time, he said, "O sage, at present I have nothing that I possess. Please grant me a one month to arrange for your *dakshina.*" Faced by such a humble request, the sage could not deny his plea and gave him a period of one month to pay the *dakshina.*

Harishchandra wandered around many towns, trying to earn enough money to give to the sage. It seemed like even fate was against him, for he was unsuccessful wherever he went. Finally, he reached the holy city of Kashi, which is today known as Varanasi.

Kashi was a large town, where many scholarly people came to gain spiritual knowledge. Pilgrims also visited in large numbers to offer their prayers to God and to their ancestors who had passed away. Even in this crowded city, Harishchandra was unable to find employment.

The grace period was ending, and Harishchandra was concerned. He could not bear to break his word, and yet he could not find a way to honor it either. Finally, his wife, who was as righteous as her husband was, made a suggestion. "My lord," she said, "In just a few days, the sage will arrive asking for his *dakshina*. We have so far been unable to make a single penny. Though it sounds improper, I have a suggestion. There is the only way left for us. There is a great demand in this city for slaves, who can work for the many rich people who live here. Please sell me and use the money to fulfill your word to the sage. Later, when you make enough money, you can buy me back again."

Harishchandra was aghast at this suggestion. "Sell my wife who has stood by me through all my troubles. Impossible!" However, as time passed, and he was unable to earn money, he had to give in to his wife's advice. With a heavy heart, he finally agreed to sell her.

Taking his wife to the slave market, he sold her to the highest bidder, an aged brahmin who agreed to pay extra for the little boy accompanying her. Faced with no choice, Harishchandra accepted the money and let his wife and child go with the brahmin. Just then, Vishwamitra arrived and demanded his *dakshina* again, and Harishchandra handed over all the money he had just received. However, Vishwamitra was not satisfied. He said, "Is this the *dakshina* you offer to a sage of my repute? I cannot accept such a meager amount! You must give me more money."

Harishchandra now decided to sell himself to raise more money. He went back to the marketplace where he had sold his wife and child and offered himself for sale. Soon, a man from the cremation ground arrived, and said he was looking for an able-bodied person to work for him. Harishchandra was sad at his own fate. One who was a king would have to work at the cremation ground now.

How low was the state he had fallen to! As these thoughts passed his mind, he realized that he had no other option, and agreed to work for the man. Vishwamitra was finally satisfied with the money he received and left.

The *chandal,* or owner of the cremation ground, who had bought Harishchandra, taught him how to cremate bodies, how much to charge for cremations, and so on. Harishchandra started living in the cremation ground, working conscientiously, though with a heavy heart.

He was continuously troubled by concern for his wife and son. He thought worriedly, "What condition will they be in? Are they waiting for me to come and rescue them? They do not even know that I am a slave myself."

Time passed, and Harishchandra was used to the work. His wife and son too got used to the poverty and the hard life they led, working in the brahmin's house. One day, Rohitashwa went to the garden to play, was bitten by a snake and died. His mother was inconsolable. She cried and cried, but finally she had to agree to consign the body to flames. She begged the brahmin for whom she toiled day and night for money, but he refused. Dejected, she went to the cremation ground with her child in her arms.

Harishchandra was on duty at the cremation ground, and he saw the woman bring a child for cremation. Poverty and difficulty had changed both of them so much, that they did not even recognize each other. As per his duty, Harishchandra asked for the payment to do the cremation. His wife began crying, saying, "I am a slave and have nothing except these clothes on my body. Even my only child is dead. What can I pay you?" Harishchandra was moved by her piteous cry, but he would not budge from his duty of collecting the charge.

Suddenly he noticed that the woman was wearing a *mangalsutra*, or symbol of her marriage, around her neck. He said, "Woman, why do you lie when you say you have nothing to give? You can give me your *mangalsutra* as fees for the cremation."

His wife was astonished. Her *mangalsutra* was a special one that could only be seen by her husband. She burst into tears, and said, "My Lord, we must have committed many sins in our previous lives to be in this state today. I am your wife, but you do not recognize me. This is our son, who is a prince, but now lies dead, without the benefit of cremation."

When his wife spoke thus, Harishchandra recognized her, and wept for his dear son. His heart was filled with agony. Yet, he would not budge. "It is my duty to collect this tax, and I shall never fail my duty, no matter what happens," he said.

She said, "All I have are the clothes on my body. Will you accept half of them and cremate our child?" When Harishchandra agreed, she started tearing off her clothes. Just then, the owner of the cremation ground appeared and said, "Your test is over Harishchandra."

The skies opened and all the celestial gods erupted in applause. The heaven rained flowers on the couple, and Vishwamitra appeared. He said, "O King, all the troubles you have faced have been created by God to test your commitment to the ideal of truthfulness and honesty. You have not only emerged victorious in these tests, but have also earned an eternal place in the hearts of people as the "Truthful One."

You may now return to your kingdom with your wife and son and continue to rule till it is time to go to the divine abode of God." As the sage said these words, the little boy lying dead on the pyre sat up and rubbed his eyes, as if waking from sleep.

Harishchandra was thrilled to see his son alive, and glad to

hear that his troubles were ending. Still, he said, "O sage, you might have given me these troubles to test me, but the fact remains that I am the slave of the owner of this crematorium and my wife is the slave of a brahmin. While we remain slaves, we cannot accept anything."

The sage was very happy. He said, "Harishchandra, you are indeed the most truthful and honest man who has ever lived. Look, there is the *chandal* and the brahmin. Indeed, the *chandal* and brahmin were present, but suddenly, their forms changed.

As they approached, the king realized that the brahmin was Indra and the *chandal* was Yamraj. They said, "We took these forms to test you, Harishchandra. Please forgive us and consider yourself free. You may now rule your kingdom in peace."

Harishchandra went back to Ayodhya. His subjects were thrilled to learn about the return of their favorite son and king. Everyone in the kingdom came to Ayodhya to celebrate their beloved king's arrival with the queen and the crown prince. Harischandra ruled righteously for many years. When the time came for him to leave earth, he handed over the reins of the kingdom to Rohitashwa.

The story of the truthful king has inspired many and continues to inspire people even today to lead a path of truthfulness. If the king can withstand enormous struggles to abide by his principles, surely we can fight the temptations in our lives and overcome difficulties in following the righteous path. Indeed, the king and his legend are truly immortal! The name "Harishchandra" has become synonymous with truthfulness and integrity.

King Bali

Bali, the king of the demons, was the great grandson of Prahlad, one of the greatest devotees of Lord Vishnu. Unlike most of the other demons, Bali was a devotee of the Lord, and was known as a just and kind ruler. He was righteous and truthful, and ruled his kingdom well. There was peace, prosperity and happiness all around.

Bali extended his reign to conquer the three worlds, including the throne of Indra, the celestial king of heaven. Seeking to take over Indra's position permanently, Bali started conducting fire sacrifices, known as the *Ashwamedha Yagna*. Indra was now worried, for if Bali succeeded in completing one hundred *Ashwamedha Yagnas*, he would be successful, and Indra would lose his position forever.

Indra approached Lord Vishnu, and pleaded that He stop Bali. However, Lord Vishnu refused. "Bali is a righteous king, and he has not committed any sins. Besides, he is a devotee of mine. How can I go and stop him from performing the sacrifices?" he asked.

Indra implored him to consider, with the plea that the associates of Bali were demons, and so this would lead to an increase of evil if he reigned permanently in heaven. Finally, Lord Vishnu agreed, saying that he would neither kill nor punish Bali, but would cut down his powers and get back Indra's kingdom.

In time, Lord Vishnu was born to Aditi, wife of Sage Kashyap, and mother of the celestial gods. He had the form of a dwarf, and came to be known as "Vaman", a Sanskrit word for dwarf. Thus, Lord Vishnu descended as Vaman. Sage Kashyap was thrilled at his good fortune, and performed the ceremony investing Him with the sacred thread.

Carrying an umbrella and a *kamandal* (small jar of water), wearing the simple garb of a brahmin boy, Vaman proceeded to the place where Emperor Bali was performing the yagna to establish his supremacy over heaven and earth. In those days, it was the custom to give cows, clothes and money to Pundits in charity while performing a yagna, and many Pundits had gathered at the site to accept the offerings.

Vaman joined a group of brahmins and awaited his turn, but his luster shone among them, and was noticed by Shukracharya, the guru of the demons. Shukracharya realized that something was amiss, and suspected that the lustrous brahmin boy was none other than Lord Vishnu Himself. He warned Bali immediately, asking him to adjourn for the day and not give anything in charity. However, Bali said, "Guruji, even if it is Lord Vishnu Himself who has come to test me or take away all that I have, I shall be thrilled to do His bidding."

Finally, it was Vaman's turn to accept charity. As soon as Bali set eyes on Him, he felt blessed. Bowing in reverence, he spoke his desire. "O great one, your beautiful face shines like the sun. I shall consider it my good fortune to give you what you desire. Please let me know what would be of use to you. Can I give you cows, or do you need gold coins, or is it silken clothes that you want? Please do not hesitate to ask me," he said very humbly.

Vaman replied, "O great King, I do not desire any of these things. I do not have need for silken robes or gold coins. Cows may be useful to me, but I have no place to keep them. I have no land to call my own, and so I beg you to give me a bit of land."

Bali laughed, "O young Pundit! I can bequeath you as many acres of land as you wish." But before he could complete, Vaman had interrupted him, "O King! I do not desire acres and acres of land. All I want is three steps of land that I can measure with my own feet. That is enough for me."

Hearing this, the whole assembly laughed. The lad was so tiny, and yet he only desired three steps of land, and that too, measured by his tiny feet! Only Shukracharya was wary. Sensing trouble, he once more warned Bali against giving him. However, Bali said, "I have given my word. No matter what he asks, I shall grant it. Please do not interfere."

He turned to Vaman, trying to convince him to accept more. Seeing him adamant, he picked up the water vessel to seal the charity. Shukracharya made one last effort to stop Bali, and taking the form of a bee, entered the vessel, blocking its mouth. When the water did not flow out, Vaman took a blade of *darbha* (sacred) grass, and pierced the mouth of the vessel. It pricked Shukracharya in one eye, and the pain forced him out of the vessel. Water flowed freely, and sipping the water from his palm, Bali confirmed his resolve to give Vaman the land he wanted.

As people looked on, the dwarf Vaman began growing, and steadily grew until he touched the skies. As everyone looked up, Vaman encompassed the whole earth with his first step. With his second step, He covered the heavens. Two of the three worlds gained, Vaman looked down at Bali and said, "O King! I have taken two steps, but I cannot find place to keep the third. You have promised me three steps of land. If you do not give me a place to keep my third step, you will be breaking your promise. Tell me what I should do."

Bali was overwhelmed and awestruck at the turn of events, but he collected himself and said, "O Lord! I am thrilled to have the opportunity of serving you. You have already blessed me by appearing before me in this form. I do not want to incur the sin of breaking my promise. Therefore, please bestow further grace upon me and take your third step on my head."

As Bali bowed down, Vaman brought his foot down, and gently placed it on Bali's head, sanctifying him with the contact. He said, "Rise, O King! You have amply justified the belief I had in your integrity, and proved to the world that you are a true devotee. I have taken away two of the three worlds you have conquered, but you still have the nether regions. Go there with your clan, and rule as wisely and as well as you have ruled the earth and the heavens. Since you performed these sacrifices righteously aspired and to become Indra, I also grant you the boon that you shall be born as Indra in another *Manvantar*." Saying this, Vaman disappeared, having completed his mission.

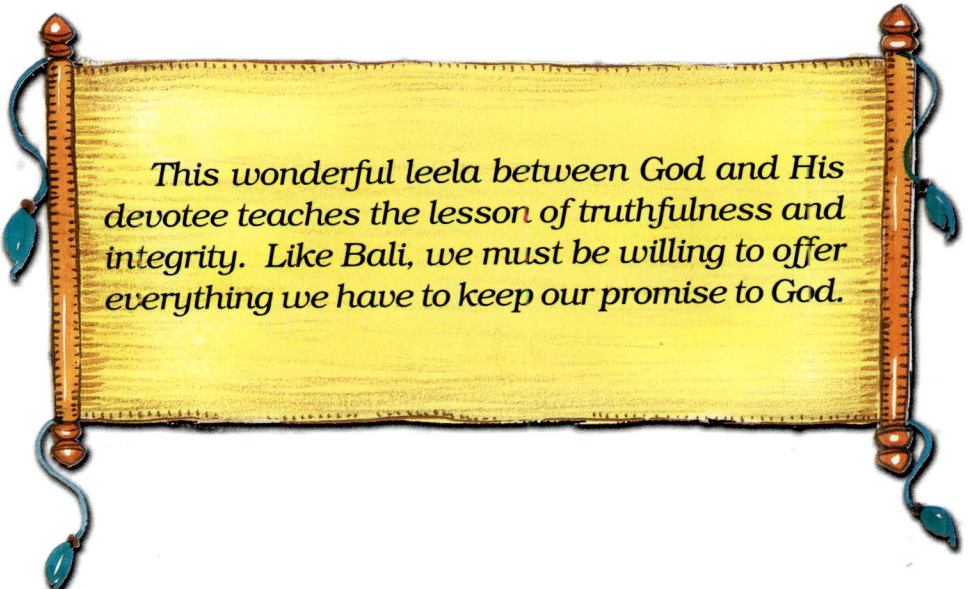

This wonderful leela between God and His devotee teaches the lesson of truthfulness and integrity. Like Bali, we must be willing to offer everything we have to keep our promise to God.

P for Perseverance

The Kripalu Value beginning with the letter "P" is Perseverance. The various aspects of perseverance are:

- ❖ Hardworking
- ❖ Enduring
- ❖ Patient
- ❖ Dedication to the work at hand
- ❖ Tenacity to bear difficulties and not give up
- ❖ Overcoming obstacles through persistence
- ❖ Keeping a positive "I can do it" attitude
- ❖ Single-mindedness towards goal
- ❖ Using tact, intelligence and mental power to solve a problem

Arjun Passes The Test

Dronacharya was one of the greatest warriors of his time. He had learned the secret of powerful weapons from the great Parashuram himself. When he arrived at Hastinapur to meet his brother-in-law, Kripacharya, Bheeshma entrusted the Pandavas and the Kauravas to his care and asked him to teach the art of weaponry to them.

The Pandavas and the Kauravas were quick to learn, and soon picked up various skills. While all the princes learned the use of all the weapons, each of them had their own favorites. While Duryodhan and Bheem favored the mace, Yudhishthir's choice of weapon was the spear. Bows and arrows fascinated Arjun, and the twins Nakul and Sahadev were most comfortable with swords.

While Dronacharya was an impartial teacher and treated all the students equally, he could not help admiring Arjun the most. Arjun was not only the finest archer, he was also the most focused, enthusiastic and resolute amongst all of Dronacharya's students. However, the Kauravas misconstrued this admiration as favoritism, and they continually complained about it.

Dronacharya decided that it was time to prove Arjun's uniqueness to the rest of the students and remove their misunderstanding. He called them to the grove at the edge of the

ashram. There, he had placed a wooden bird with a prominently painted eye on a tree. He then addressed all the students, "Young princes, you have learned most of the skills necessary for a warrior, and it is time you take a test to prove your abilities. I want you to show me your skill in archery. On that tree is a wooden bird with a painted eye. Please take aim at the eye of the bird."

All the Pandava and Kaurava princes held their bows and aimed their arrows at the target before them. Dronacharya first questioned Duryodhan, "What do you see?" Duryodhan replied, "Gurudev, I see the bird, the tree, and I also see Bheem standing here." Dronacharya then asked Bheem, "What do you see?" Bheem replied, "I see the bird, its eye, the tree, and its fruits and leaves." Yudhishthir was questioned next, "What do you see?" He said, "Guruji, I see the bird and its eye."

Finally, Dronacharya turned to Arjun and asked, "What do you see?" Arjun replied, "Gurudev, I see only the eye of the bird and nothing else." With a smile on his face, Dronacharya said, "Now hit the target!" Arjun shot the arrow and hit the mark.

Dronacharya turned to the other princes and said, "Did you understand the point of this test? When you aim at a target, you must concentrate all your attention on it. Intense absorption of your physical and mental faculties on the task you perform is the key to success. When I asked you all to aim at the eye of the bird, the rest of you were seeing other things as well, like the tree, its fruits and leaves, and the people around, because you were not concentrating singularly on your target. Only Arjun was totally focused. Now you know why I am so fond of Arjun." Dronacharya's test silenced the Kauravas, and all understood that Arjun was indeed the best student.

There is another story that also illustrates the perseverance of Arjun. Bheem was a voracious eater, and ate often during the day. Sometimes, he woke up hungry at night and continued to

eat. One day,
Arjun woke up
in the middle of
the night and
heard sounds of
Bheem eating,
even though it was
pitch dark and
nothing could be
seen.

At first, he
was surprised
that   his
brother could eat in such
darkness, but he soon realized
that if one tried hard, with
practice one could adapt the eyes
to darkness. This made him realize
that he could practice archery in the
darkness, and he immediately began
working towards that goal.

To use a bow and arrow in the
darkness was no easy task, and hitting

a target under such conditions would be stupendous. However, with his diligence and perseverance, Arjun soon mastered this skill. He was one of the few archers who were as good with a bow and arrow at night as in the daytime.

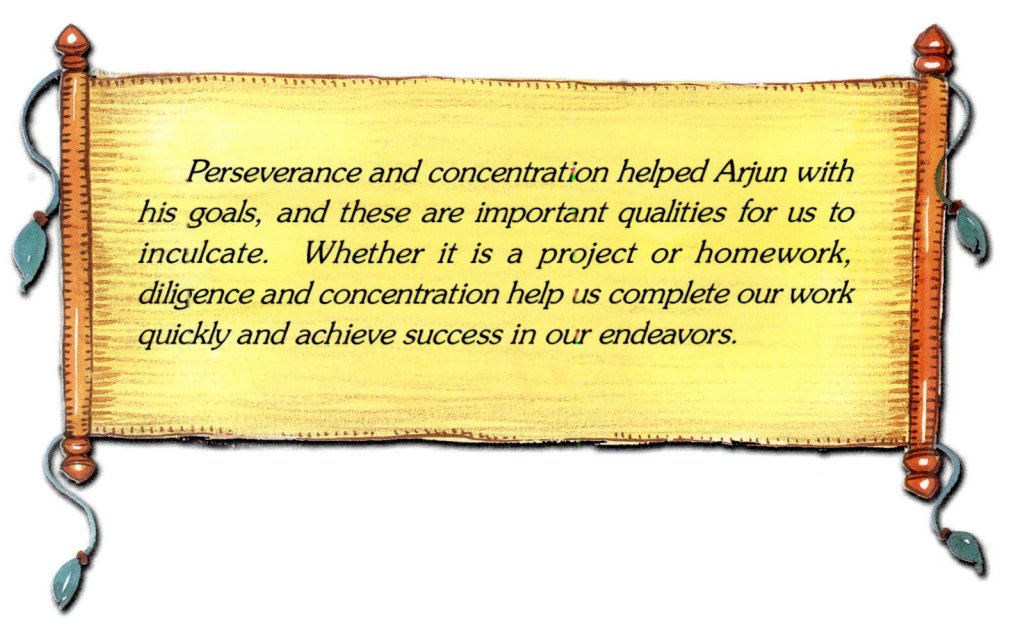

Perseverance and concentration helped Arjun with his goals, and these are important qualities for us to inculcate. Whether it is a project or homework, diligence and concentration help us complete our work quickly and achieve success in our endeavors.

Abhimanyu

Abhimanyu, the son of Arjun, was as brave and skilled as his illustrious father. Though he was one of the youngest warriors in the great battle of Mahabharat, he carved a name for himself by his valiant deeds.

Arjun was married to Subhadra, the sister of Shree Krishna. Her Divine brother enjoyed recounting tales of his days at the *gurukul*, and she was always a keen listener. One day, while she was pregnant, Shree Krishna related the story of how he had learnt the secret of the *Chakravyuh*, a complex wheel-like army formation, which is extremely difficult to penetrate. Once inside the formation, it is even more difficult to exit.

Subhadra was tired, and after a short while, she dropped off to sleep, while Shree Krishna continued to talk. However, the child in her womb was interested in learning, and continued to listen. He learned the secret of entering the formation. After some time, Shree Krishna realized that His sister had fallen asleep, and He stopped the narration. The child was upset and woke up his mother. It was too late, for Shree Krishna would not continue the narration. Thus the child, who grew up to be Abhimanyu, learnt the secret of entering the *Chakravyuh*, but did not learn how to break free from it.

Abhimanyu spent his childhood in Dwaraka with his maternal family, since the Pandavas were in exile in the forest. Once the period of exile was over, they spent a year in hiding, in the kingdom of Virat. At the end of the year, the king of Virat, overjoyed at his acquaintance with the Pandavas, offered his daughter Uttara in marriage to Arjun. However, Arjun had been the dance

teacher of Uttara during the year, and so he looked upon her as his daughter. He accepted her as his daughter-in-law – Abhimanyu's wife. Thus, Abhimanyu was married at an early age, but he scarcely had time to spend with his father or his new bride, for the Mahabharat war soon began between the Kauravas and the Pandavas. The young warrior refused to stay home, and chose to fight in the war, against expert warriors who were much older and more experienced than he was.

Abhimanyu fought bravely and immediately won the admiration of his elders. As the battle ensued, he was considered a serious threat to the Kaurava army. The thirteenth day of the battle dawned with Arjun busy in a far corner of the battlefield. Dronacharya, the Kaurava commander, arrayed his army in the *Chakravyuh* formation, well aware that none but Arjun would be able to break it. Yudhishthir was at a loss, knowing that his inability to break the formation would lead to massive losses for them. He then turned to Abhimanyu and asked him to lead the army and enter the *Chakravyuh*.

The young, inexperienced lad replied, "Uncle, I will be happy to lead the army and enter the formation, but there is just one thing. I can break through the *Chakravyuh*, but I do not know how to come out of it. I am not worried about losing my life, but I will not be able to contain the army single handedly." Yudhishthir was happy with his brave nephew's answer, and said, "Son, you will not be alone, for all of us will be right behind you and will enter the formation after you succeed in breaking it. We shall fight together and manage to escape after wreaking havoc to the enemy."

Thus encouraged, the brave young lad took charge and led the army straight towards Dronacharya at the head of the formation. He charged at the commander-in-chief of the Kaurava army, breaching the fortification. The Kauravas had been prepared for just such an assault, and they succeeded in closing the breach almost as soon as it opened. Abhimanyu was left all alone inside the formation, surrounded by the best warriors among the Kauravas – Karn, Duryodhan, Dushasan, Dronacharya, Ashwatthama, and many others.

The young warrior faced all of them in the battle single-handedly and bravely. His skill drew even the seasoned warriors' grudging appreciation. He made the best use of all the arts he had learned from his uncle Shree Krishna, and from his father Arjun, and managed to smother the best of the Kaurava forces.

Duryodhan was enraged when he saw the skill of his sworn enemy's son, and at Dronacharya's appreciation of his mastery over the art of war. He reminded Dronacharya of his duty towards the Kaurava forces and prodded him to perform his duty and defeat the enemy. Much against his will, Dronacharya brought all his experience and skill to the fore, and systematically broke down Abhimanyu's resistance.

Surrounded by warriors on all sides, Abhimanyu did not give up, but fought valiantly. In an epic climax on the thirteenth day of the war, a pitched battle between the brave young lion, Abhimanyu and the Kaurava forces unfolded.

Karn, encouraged by Dronacharya, strategically broke Abhimanyu's chariot. Undaunted, Abhimanyu stood on the ground, bow in hand. When his bow was also broken by Karn, Abhimanyu picked up a sword and shield. Unfazed, he wielded his sword with amazing skill at his opponents who showered a rain of arrows on the exposed prince. When the sword broke, he took a spear to fight his unfair enemies. Even when all his weapons were lost, he picked up one of the wheels of his broken chariot and used it like a discus, and faced many enemies at once.

At last, the wheel broke, but Abhimanyu was not through. He engaged Dushasan's son in mortal combat with a mace. Against the rules of warfare, his opponent carried weapons, while Abhimanyu had none, and he ultimately met his tragic end.

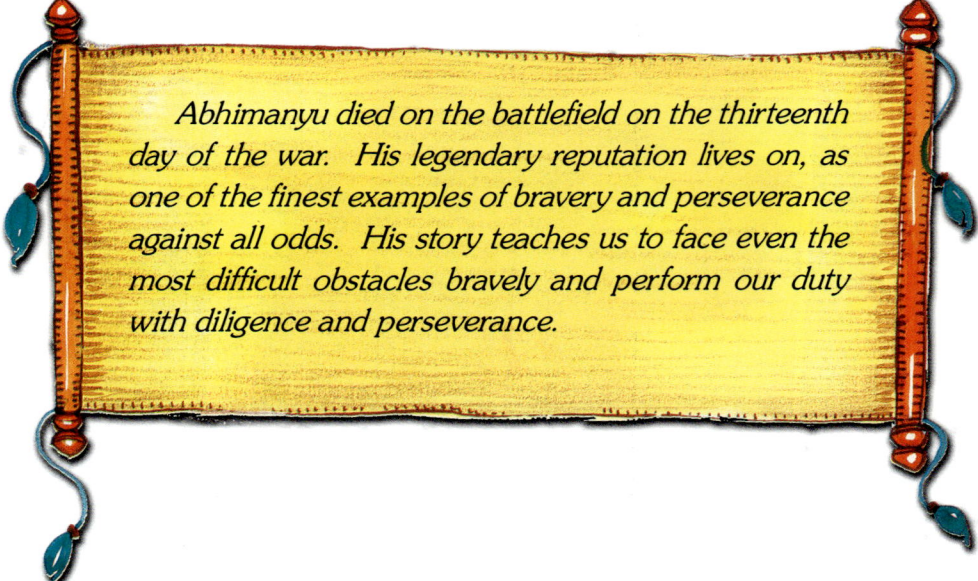

Abhimanyu died on the battlefield on the thirteenth day of the war. His legendary reputation lives on, as one of the finest examples of bravery and perseverance against all odds. His story teaches us to face even the most difficult obstacles bravely and perform our duty with diligence and perseverance.

Nachiketa

The Kathopanishad deals with the complex matter of life and death, in the simple manner of a dialogue between the god of death Yamraj and a little boy named Nachiketa. The story of Nachiketa is an inspiring one, and is what forms the basis of the entire Kathopanishad.

Nachiketa was the son of a King Vajashrava. Once, Vajashrava performed a sacrifice called Vishvajit. In that sacrifice, one has to give away everything one possesses. Nothing is to be kept back. Being a miser, he sought an easy way out, by donating old and weak cows that were past their milk-bearing stage. Nachiketa saw this and was deeply disturbed by the stinginess of his father.

He attempted to speak to his father, reminding him of the effect of his wrongdoing. Vajashrava turned a deaf ear to his son's wise counsel. Nachiketa did not give up, and instead asked his father, "I too am your property; a property that does not yield any returns. Whom will you donate me too?" This question annoyed Vajashrava so much that he finally lost his patience and shouted, "I bequeath you to Yamraj, the god of death." Nachiketa was undisturbed by his father's outburst. Yamraj presided over the nether regions, called Yamlok, and Nachiketa decided to go there, as commanded by his father.

As soon as Vajashrava realized what had happened, he repented for his anger as well his greed, and tried to persuade Nachiketa to stay back. However, Nachiketa was firm in his intent. He had been given to Yamraj in charity by the utterance of his father, and he would gladly go to the abode of death in fulfillment of his father's declaration.

Nachiketa reached Yamlok, only to find that the Yamraj was out, and would not return for three days. The guards refused to let him enter the palace in the absence of their master. The little boy spent three days and nights outside the palace gates of Yamraj, without a morsel of food or a drop of water. What endurance by a child who was barely seven!

When Yamraj returned, he was astonished to see a child waiting for him at his doorstep, and was aghast when he learnt that no one had even offered him food or water for three days. He reprimanded his wife and servants, and ordered them to take care of Nachiketa at once. He himself took the little boy inside and fed him with the choicest delicacies, and made him comfortable.

However, he still felt guilty of inappropriately treating a guest, and in an effort to make up for it, he said, "Nachiketa, I have sinned by making a brahmin child like you wait without food or water. Please allow me to atone for it by offering you three boons. Ask for whatever you wish, and I shall give it."

Nachiketa explained the situation to Yamraj and said that as per his father's word, he now belonged to Yamraj and that he would stay back in Yamlok as his servant. However, Yamraj assured him that he was relieved from his bondage, and insisted that he ask for three boons. Finally, Nachiketa replied, "Sir, thank you for welcoming me so warmly, setting me free of bondage, and offering me the boons. My first wish is that when I return home, my father should welcome me without any resentment." Yamraj replied, "Let it be so." Nachiketa then said, "My second wish is

that you teach me that knowledge by which one may go to heaven." Yamraj was pleased, and taught him the secrets of *yagyas,* or ritualistic fire sacrifices, as described in the Vedas for the attainment of heaven. Nachiketa learnt this so fast and easily, that Yamraj declared, "The fire in the *yagya* will henceforth be known by your name, as 'Nachiketa Agni'."

It was the turn for the third and final boon. Nachiketa asked to be taught how to attain immortality through the knowledge of the soul and God. Yamraj was astonished that a little boy could desire such profound knowledge, and tried to dissuade him by offering worldly wealth and heavenly pleasures instead. However, Nachiketa was steadfast. He said, "I have no desire for these things. You are the only one who can reveal Divine knowledge to me, and this is all I now I seek from you." Finally, Yamraj realized that this little boy was an elevated soul, and was eligible for Divine knowledge. He taught Nachiketa *brahmagyan*, or the Supreme Absolute Truth.

Thus, Nachiketa became enlightened, and when he returned, his father and the *rishis* (sages) of the kingdom, warmly welcomed him. He grew up to become a great *rishi* himself and finally, attaining release from the cycle of life and death, went to the abode of God.

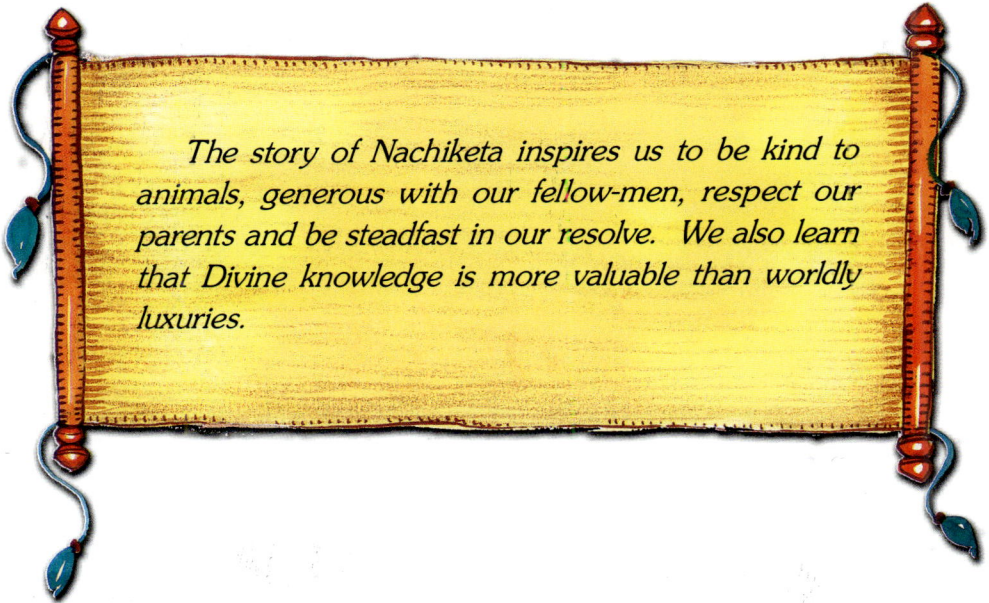

The story of Nachiketa inspires us to be kind to animals, generous with our fellow-men, respect our parents and be steadfast in our resolve. We also learn that Divine knowledge is more valuable than worldly luxuries.

A for Accountability

The Kripalu value beginning with the letter "A" is Accountability. The various aspects of integrity are:

- ❖ Taking full responsibility for ones deeds
- ❖ Taking the onus for mistakes and the responsibility for correcting them
- ❖ not blaming others or having a whining nature,
- ❖ Taking responsibility for organizing oneself and one's work
- ❖ Accepting the law of karma that what happens to us is a result of our own actions
- ❖ Being punctual to our time commitments

Valmiki

Thousands of years ago, lived a robber by the name of Ratnakar. He was a dreaded dacoit who robbed anyone passing through the jungle. Stealing and looting were the only things he knew, and he raised his family by such means. One day, the great sage Narad was passing through and was accosted by Ratnakar, who ordered him to hand over all his possessions.

Narad smiled and said, "Dear man, I have nothing but the tanpura (a musical instrument) that I hold in my hand. Of what use are worldly possessions to me? I roam around the three worlds singing the glories of God." Ratnakar was stunned by this attitude, and wanted to know more about the wise man.

The sage, with his divine vision, realized that this was the time to awaken Ratnakar from his sinful ways, and asked him why he robbed wayfarers. Ratnakar replied simply, "To feed and clothe my family." The sage said, "You steal and kill to help your family. But it is you who will have to pay for these actions, not your family." Ratnakar disagreed, saying that his family would certainly understand that his actions were performed for them, and they would share the fruits too. Narad challenged Ratnakar to go and ask his family if they would share the results of his sinful actions.

Ratnakar agreed, and going home, he put forth the question to his family members. His parents refused to accept the sins, saying that it was his responsibility to provide for them, and the method he used had nothing to do with them. His wife said that her duty was to cook food at home, while his duty was to earn money. If he committed sins to fulfill his duty, he alone was responsible for them, and she would not share the fruits. His children said that as a father it was his duty to teach them right and wrong, and not to pass the fruits of his sinful deeds to them.

A different Ratnakar returned to the waiting sage. His eyes were opened and the bonds of attachment were broken forever. Narad was pleased to see the change, and instructed him to chant "Ram," the Divine Name of the Lord. However, Ratnakar had committed so many sins that the name of God would not come to his lips. Narad then asked him to chant the word "Mara," the reverse of "Ram." He asked Ratnakar to continue chanting until he returned.

Ratnakar obeyed his Guru's instructions with full faith, and sat down to chant "Mara Mara." He did not even interrupt the chanting to get up, lie down, eat or drink. Many years went by, and his body dried up. Termites built an anthill around him. The sage Narad returned to see how his disciple was faring and saw that Ratnakar was so deep in meditation that termites had eaten away into his body. Yet, he had not stopped his chanting!

Narad then blessed him with the vision of God, and revived his body. Since Ratnakar had emerged from an anthill, which is called *valmik* in Sanskrit, then onwards came to be known by the name Valmiki.

Valmiki was curious about the ideal personality. "Who could be considered the epitome of virtue and wisdom in this world?" Sage Narad then told him about how God would descend in the

world as Lord Ram, the king of Ayodhya, and demonstrate perfect virtues and wisdom, from an early age.

Moved by this story, Valmiki continued thinking about it long after Narad had left. While walking to the river Tamasa for his daily ablutions, his eyes fell on a pair of mating *Krauncha* (Heron) birds. He paused to savor the moment and share their happiness. Suddenly, an arrow released by a hunter shattered the calm, and the male bird fell dead. The female bird cried over her loss in a heart-rending manner, which moved the sage to pity. Catching sight of the hunter who had separated the loving birds, Valmiki cursed him, "You have separated these birds that were deeply in love. Never in your life will you be able to rest; you shall wander homeless all your life."

No sooner had he cursed the man that he regretted his action, realizing that he had succumbed to a fit of anger. As Valmiki recalled his words, he realized that the words he had spoken in fury had taken the form of a *shlok*, or Sanskrit verse, which rhymed with the wailing of the bereaved *Krauncha* bird.

Valmiki realized that it was the will of God, which made him utter those words. Concluding that there must have been a reason for this occurrence, he went into meditation. Brahma soon appeared in front of him, and said, "Son, these events have taken place to help you begin writing the story of Lord Ram. It is time the world learned of the divine pastimes of Lord Ram, one of the avatars of God." Brahma gave Valmiki special vision which enabled him to see the events as they would occur in the future, so that he could write down the story in great detail.

Valmiki then composed the Ramayan in the format of *shlokas*, or verses. In it, Valmiki described the divine virtues and wonderful

pastimes of Lord Ram even before they were manifested on earth.

Valmiki was acclaimed as a great rishi, and he set up his ashram on the banks of the Ganga. Later, during the avatar of Lord Ram, Valmiki himself became part of the Ramayan, when he gave refuge to Seeta and took her children as his disciples.

Shree Ram and Seeta's children, Luv and Kush, learnt the Ramayan from Valmiki, their Guru. When they sang it in the court of Shree Ram, even He was moved by the beautiful narration of His own story.

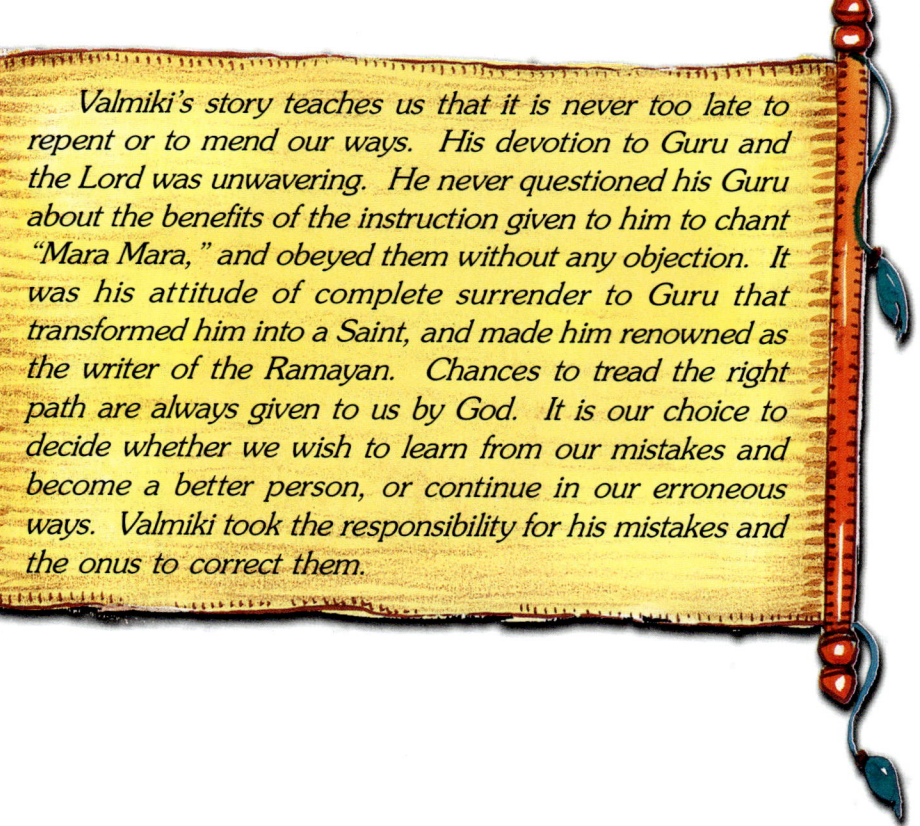

Valmiki's story teaches us that it is never too late to repent or to mend our ways. His devotion to Guru and the Lord was unwavering. He never questioned his Guru about the benefits of the instruction given to him to chant "Mara Mara," and obeyed them without any objection. It was his attitude of complete surrender to Guru that transformed him into a Saint, and made him renowned as the writer of the Ramayan. Chances to tread the right path are always given to us by God. It is our choice to decide whether we wish to learn from our mistakes and become a better person, or continue in our erroneous ways. Valmiki took the responsibility for his mistakes and the onus to correct them.

L for Love for God

The Kripalu Value beginning with the letter "L" is love for God. The various aspects of Love for God are:

- ❖ Trust in God
- ❖ Faith in His protection
- ❖ Acceptance of His will
- ❖ Keeping a positive attitude in every situation with faith in God's Grace
- ❖ A sense of gratitude for all that God has given us
- ❖ Belief that He is with us and watching us always
- ❖ Doing all actions for His pleasure
- ❖ unconditional devotion to Him

Markandeya

Mrikandu was a great sage and an ardent devotee of Lord Shiv. He and his wife Marudvati dedicated their life to the worship of the Lord, and their only regret was that they had no child to whom they could pass on their devotion.

In response to his prayers, Lord Shiv appeared before Mrikandu, and said, "I am very pleased with you and your wife. I have decided to grant your dearest wish of bearing a child. However, you have a choice. Do you want a son who will be smart and intelligent, but will only live for sixteen years, or do you want a foolish son with a long life?" Mrikandu replied immediately, "Lord, we would rather have an intelligent son, even if his life will be short. Of what use is a long life if one is not intelligent enough to make use of it for the right purpose?" Lord Shiv was pleased by Mrikandu's choice, and left, granting the sage his wish.

A child was born to Marudvati and they named him "Markandeya," literally meaning "the son of Mrikandu." Even as a child, he stood out among the other children of his father's *ashram,* with his divine luster that grew as he absorbed knowledge like a sponge. At a young age, his father performed his thread ceremony and started teaching him the Vedas and the Puranas. The child picked up the mantras easily, amazing the inmates of the ashram. In a few years, he had mastered all the Vedas and the Shastras, making his parents proud.

As his sixteenth birthday drew near, Sage Mrikandu and Marudvati became anxious, remembering Lord's injunction, and fearing that they would lose their son whom they adored so much. Markandeya noticed his parents' apprehension, and asked them the reason for their sadness. Sage Mrikandu explained the circumstances of his birth, the conditions laid down by Lord Shiv, and his approaching death. "My son, we were so happy at the

prospect of getting an intelligent son, that we did not worry about the short life span. Now, we cannot bear to be parted from you, and are worried about what will happen just a few days from now."

Markandeya smiled and replied, "Father, you have taught me the Vedas, the Puranas and the Shastras. You have taught me that the Lord always listens to the sincere prayers of his devotees. Please do not worry. It is Lord Shiv who has decreed that I should live for sixteen years. I shall pray to him, and ask him to extend my life. He will surely answer my sincere prayers." Speaking thus, with a confident smile, Markandeya went to the riverbank, made a *Shiv Ling* with sand, and began praying with all his heart.

Days passed, and Markandeya was immersed in his prayers, when Yamraj, the god of Death, arrived to take his soul from his mortal body. Seeing the fearful form of Yamraj, Markandeya tightly hugged the *Shiv Ling* he had made. Yamraj laughed and said, "Child, it is my duty to take you today. Nothing and no one can save you now." Saying this, he threw his noose over the boy, but he was so close to the *Ling* that the noose encircled the *Shiv Ling* and Markandeya.

As soon as the noose touched the *Shiv Ling*, Lord Shiv was enraged. He burst out of it, and kicked Yamraj. "How dare you throw your noose on me," he shouted, shocking Yamraj. Caught off-guard, Yamraj tried to explain that it was his duty, but Lord Shiv was furious. He said, "This boy has come to me for protection, and he shall have it. Yamraj, you can never touch him as he will be immortal." Chastised and disappointed, Yamraj left for his abode. Lord Shiv blessed Markandeya with a long life, and with immense knowledge. Markandeya returned home, making his parents ecstatic. He went on to become one of the most learned *rishis* of all time.

There are many powerful hymns, such as the Maha Mrityunjaya mantra that protect one from death, which are ascribed to him. He is mentioned in many of the sacred epics and Puranas. The Markandeya Puran comprises of a conversation between Sage Markandeya and Sage Jaimini, and is a storehouse of knowledge and information. The Devi Mahatmaya, a treatise on the Devi, is part of this Puran. Markandeya's story and dialogues are also described in many chapters of the Shreemad Bhagavatam.

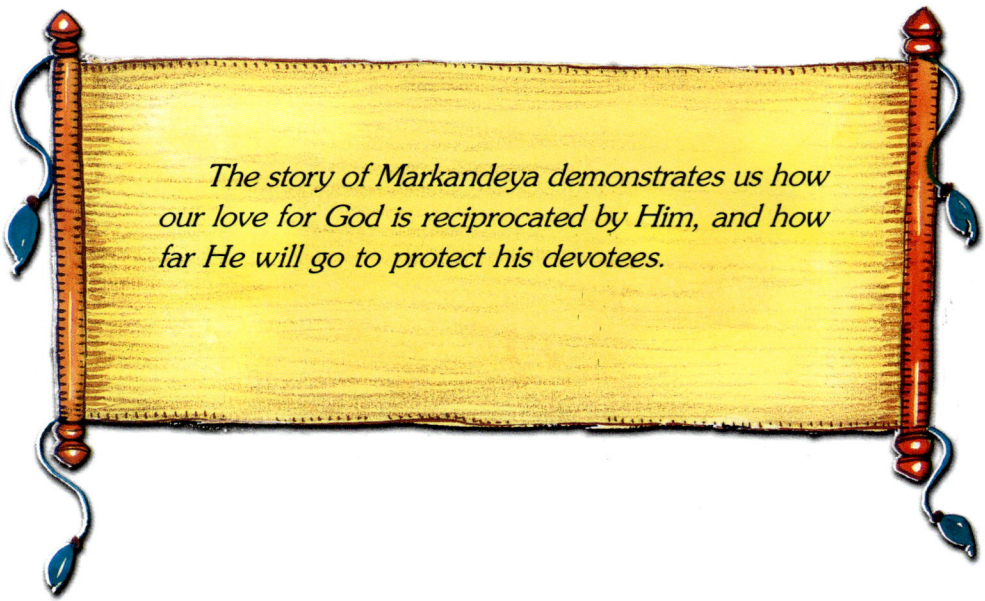

The story of Markandeya demonstrates us how our love for God is reciprocated by Him, and how far He will go to protect his devotees.

Shabari

The story of Shabari, who was born in a hunter's family, but attained selfless devotion to the lotus feet of Lord Ram is very inspiring, and is described in the great epic, the Ramayan.

Shabari was born in a poor hunter's family. Right from her childhood, she was averse to the killing of animals for

pleasure, or even for food. At her wedding, when she heard that animals would be sacrificed as a part of the ceremony, she ran away and hid in the forest. Seeking help, she arrived at the ashram of the sage Matang, who welcomed her with open arms. She was content performing the menial tasks at the ashram, and spent every minute of the day in the contemplation of God.

When the time came for Sage Matang to depart from his body, Shabari asked him to grant her salvation too. The sage replied, "Shabari, I am an unfortunate soul, whose time has come, and has to leave just when the Lord Himself is about to arrive at my doorstep. It is you who are fortunate for you will meet the Lord in his form as Shree Ram, and receive the highest treasure of Divine love directly from Him. Stay on in this ashram and wait for the day when Shree Ram will arrive here with His brother Lakshman, searching for His wife Seeta. Serve Him well, and your devotion will bear fruit." Telling her the story of Shree Ram, the sage departed, leaving Shabari alone at the ashram.

Shabari continued her tasks at the ashram, keeping it ready for Lord Ram's arrival. She awoke morning, wondering if this would be the day when Shree Ram would arrive. After completing her chores, she would make the place ready for His arrival, and collect fruits and berries for him to eat if He did come. She would taste every berry and keep aside the best and the sweetest of them for her Lord. She would spend hours removing the thorns from the bushes along the path and the stones on the path, so that her Beloved Lord would not be hurt. Thus, she spent many years waiting for her Lord who was soon to come to her abode.

Finally, the day came when Shree Ram and Lakshman arrived at the ashram while searching for Seeta, who had been abducted by the evil King Ravan. Seeing the Lord in front of her eyes, Shabari was overjoyed. She welcomed Him inside, saying that she had been eagerly waiting for Him. Making Him comfortable, she offered Him the berries she had herself tasted and found the sweetest.

Lakshman was amazed to see the old woman offering half-eaten berries to Shree Ram with such love. Lord Ram was eating them with great satisfaction, relishing the sweetness of her devotion, with which she was offering the berries. Lakshman bowed down at the feet of Shabari and said, "O mother, your love for Ram will be remembered forever in this world. I bow down in reverence to the great devotee of Shree Ram."

Shabari felt that her greatest desire had been fulfilled by meeting the Lord. Shree Ram blessed her with the gift of Divine love and transformed her from an old woman to a beautiful young woman. At the end of her life, Shabari went to the Saket Lok, the Divine abode of Lord Ram, as Sage Matang had foretold.

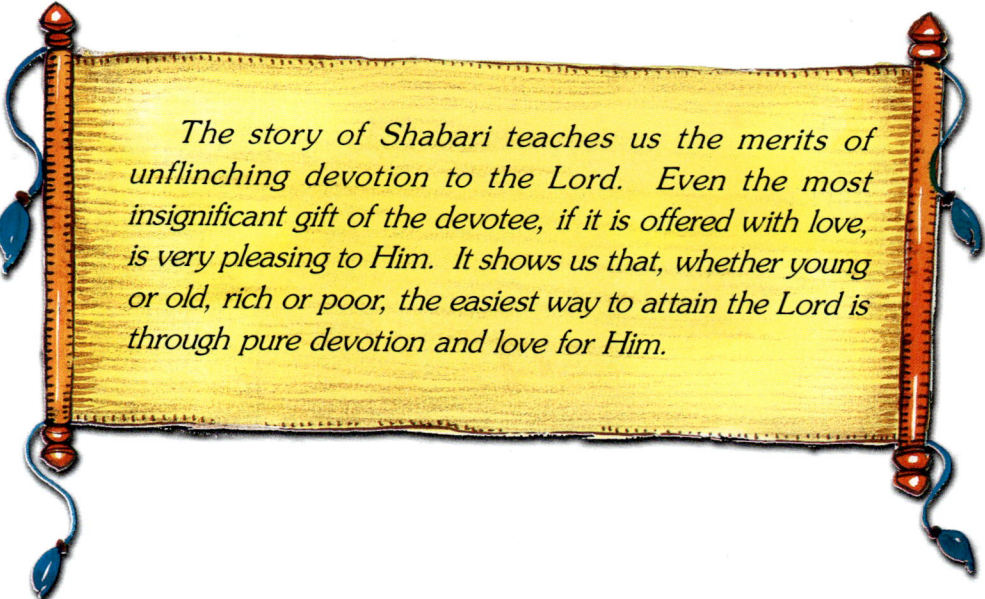

The story of Shabari teaches us the merits of unflinching devotion to the Lord. Even the most insignificant gift of the devotee, if it is offered with love, is very pleasing to Him. It shows us that, whether young or old, rich or poor, the easiest way to attain the Lord is through pure devotion and love for Him.

Draupadi

Draupadi was one of the most unfathomable personalities in the Mahabharat. Daughter of King Drupad, the king of Panchal, and the wife of the Pandavas, she was a heroic princess and queen who became well known for her great beauty as well as her strength of mind. She had to undergo great tribulations. She was both compassionate and generous to the good, but also fiery against her enemies. She was no less heroic than Arjun or Bheem, for it was she who brought about the ruin of the Kauravas, who had tried to strip her of her dignity.

She shared a very special relationship with Shree Krishna – that of friendship mixed with devotion. She considered Shree Krishna her only true friend; and He too reciprocated with her accordingly.

Once Draupadi was visiting Shree Krishna at Dwaraka, when He accidentally cut his finger. Many of His close aides were distressed to hear the news. Draupadi immediately tore off the end of her saree and tied it on Shree Krishna's finger, stemming the flow of blood. It was a little piece of cloth that Draupadi used for Shree Krishna at the time of need, but this little sacrifice was well rewarded by Shree Krishna when Draupadi was in dire straits.

Shree Krishna had to perform the work of annihilating the evil kings, and for the destruction of the Kauravas, it was Draupadi, who was his instrument. He gave her the courage to handle all the problems she had to face, coming to her aid each time. Her devotion and love for Shree Krishna were great, and she never hesitated to do what she could for Him.

Once, Duryodhan planned to cheat the Pandavas out of their kingdom of Indraprastha by inviting them to a game of dice. Yudhishthir was a skilled player, but he was no match for Shakuni,

the evil uncle of Duryodhan, who was cunning and deceitful in playing dice. Duryodhan's plan worked, and Yudhishthir lost all his possessions, his kingdom, and finally his brothers and himself. Finally, he staked Draupadi, and lost her too.

Thrilled at having the Pandavas as his slaves, Duryodhan ordered Draupadi to be dragged to the court. Yudhishthir hung his head in shame, realizing the unjustness of his action in staking his wife, but it was too late. Queen Draupadi was dragged into the court, dazed and unbelieving in the turn of events.

Draupadi was not a meek woman; she was a true queen, fiery and intense. Even as she was being dragged by Dushasan, she ridiculed him for choosing to show his prowess against her, an unarmed woman. She challenged him to do the same with her husbands, taunting him that he would not dare to take on any of her husbands in a fight.

Draupadi was knowledgeable and intelligent, and did not hesitate to take a stand against evil. In the court full of men, she challenged Yudhishtir with questions: Had he lost her before or after he had lost himself? If he had already lost himself, what right did he have to pledge her, since as a slave he had lost all rights over her? As Yudhishthir hung his head, unable to answer his wife, she turned to the old and wise men in the court. How had they allowed such an act to occur in their presence? Why had none of them protested at such an injustice? She further challenged the game itself. Why was Shakuni playing on behalf of Duryodhan? Why had Duryodhan not placed his brothers or his wife as a matching stake?

Draupadi's spirited questioning made the elders squirm in their seats, but none of them spoke up in support of her. Duryodhan grew even bolder and ordered Dushasan to disrobe Draupadi. As Dushasan dragged Draupadi by the hair to the center of the court,

she cast her pleading eyes towards her husbands for help. Since they had lost in gambling, they looked down in shame.

Draupadi then turned to the elders present – Bheeshma, Dronacharya, Kripacharya and Vidur – hoping they would rescue her from this plight. However, they too sat silently, regretting their inability to stop the wicked act. Draupadi was not willing to succumb to such humiliation. She reprimanded them all for tolerating wickedness and allowing it to flourish.

Not finding one soul in the entire court ready to come to her rescue, she turned to the only support who would never let her down – her friend and mentor, Lord Krishna. She raised her hands and called out to Him, "O Shree Krishna of Dwaraka! Please come and save me."

The Lord never abandons a devotee who considers Him as the only shelter, and so Shree Krishna did not wait a moment. As soon as Draupadi uttered His name with devotion, he came to her aid, providing unending lengths of cloth to preserve her modesty.

The wicked Dushasan was stunned to see that the length of Draupadi's saree kept miraculously increasing and clothing her, not allowing the great woman to get exposed. The more he pulled her saree, the more appeared in its place, to the growing awe of the whole court, and the utter bewilderment of the wicked Kauravas. At last, Dushasan was so tired and fatigued that he collapsed on the floor, while Draupadi stood with her head held high, surrounded by the unending yards of cloth, her gift from her Beloved friend, Lord Krishna.

This was not the only occasion Shree Krishna came to Draupadi's aid. He continued to help her, no matter when and where she remembered the Lord. Once, when the Pandavas were in exile in the forest, the sage Durvasa arrived with ten thousand

disciples. As was the custom in those days, Yudhishthir invited him to partake of food, to which the sage agreed, saying that he would eat after having a bath in the river. When Yudhishthir informed Draupadi that Durvasa and his disciples would be eating, she was crestfallen, for she had just cleaned all the vessels for the day, and there was no food remaining.

Scared at the prospect of inviting the wrath of the sage who was known for his anger, Draupadi turned to Shree Krishna again, calling out to Him with all her heart. Shree Krishna appeared at once, and mischievously asked her for food. The perturbed Draupadi showed him her cleaned vessels, from which Shree Krishna picked up a bit of rice stuck to the rim of one of them, and teased her saying that she did not know how to clean vessels. Shree Krishna ate the rice, and said, "Ah! That has satisfied my hunger. Now go and call the sage for food." Draupadi looked on in amazement, but she trusted Shree Krishna and immediately obeyed him.

Meanwhile, the sage and his disciples, emerging from their bath, suddenly felt so full and satiated that they felt they could not eat another morsel, and excusing themselves from Yudhishthir, left the forest at once.

Draupadi's story teaches us to develop the mental strength to face all sorts of trials and tribulations that life may throw at us. We should always be devoted to the Lord, and have firm faith in His protection. Draupadi never wavered from her devotion to Shree Krishna in spite of all the troubles she had to face. We must remember that the Lord protects those who depends totally upon Him.

U for Unassuming

The Kripalu value beginning with the letter "U" is Unassuming. The various aspects of being unassuming are:

- ❖ Modesty
- ❖ Unpretentiousness
- ❖ Simplicity
- ❖ Humility
- ❖ Not boasting or showing off
- ❖ Reverence for the Greatness of God
- ❖ Faith that everything belongs to God and not to us
- ❖ Realizing that God has a grand scheme why things happen and we all have a tiny role to play in His design

Parikshit

The Mahabharat War was almost over and many warriors lay dead on the battlefield. However, the hatred and anger in the hearts of the remaining Kauravas and their supporters was alive and burning.

With rage in his eyes, Ashwatthama, the son of Dronacharya[1], decided to wreak havoc upon the Pandava forces in the dead of the night. Seeking revenge against Drishtadyumna[2] for killing his father, he entered the Pandava camp while they were asleep and killed Drishtadyumna before he could awaken. Then, in a dastardly act to avenge the deaths amongst the Kauravas, he massacred all the sons of Draupadi, while they were fast asleep. The morning brought despair and grief to the Pandava forces, who had been jubilant the night before. When Shree Krishna and the Pandavas tracked down Ashwatthama, he was deep in meditation, but Ashwatthama's hatred still had not abated, for he made one last attempt to ensure that the Pandavas would have none of their dear ones left.

---

[1] *Dronacharya* – Teacher of the Kauravas and Pandavas. He became the Commander-in-chief of the Kaurava army after Bheeshma.

[2] *Drishtadyumna* – Drupad's son and Draupadi's brother. He was the Commander-in-chief of the Pandava army.

Taking up a blade of sacred *darbha* grass, he turned it into a weapon, and aimed it at the grandson of the Pandavas. The grandson was the unborn child in the womb of Uttara, the wife of Abhimanyu[3]. Shree Krishna, realizing the danger, entered the womb in a subtle form, and saved the child by absorbing the force of the weapon. This child was the only scion of the Pandavas to survive the war.

This child, son of the brave Abhimanyu, remembered the beautiful face of his savior in his mother's womb, and once he was born, tried to recognize the person. Even as a newborn, he looked searchingly at all who came to see him, earning the name "Parikshit", or the one who examines all. His eyes stopped searching the day Shree Krishna visited him, for he found the Divine person he was looking for.

Parikshit was well tutored by his grandfathers, the Pandavas, and uncle, Shree Krishna, but he was just a young boy when Shree Krishna left for His abode in Golok. The Pandavas, unable to imagine a life without the guidance of Shree Krishna, also left for His abode after crowning Parikshit as the king of Hastinapur.

The young king had all the qualities of his father and his grandfather, and ruled well with the guidance of those older and more experienced than him. It was during his reign that the age of Dwapar ended, and the age of Kali began. As soon as Parikshit heard of the advent of Kaliyug on the earth, he set out in search of it, so that he could contain it before it created havoc in his peaceful kingdom. He soon saw an old bull with three broken legs, standing on its fourth leg, while a well dressed, but evil-looking man whipped it to go faster. He tried to stop this atrocity, but the man prostrated himself before the king, saying that he was Kalyug, and supplicated for mercy. He begged for a place to live.

---

[3] *Abhimanyu* – Son of Arjun and Subhadra

The kind King Parikshit could not refuse someone who begged for mercy, so he made Kalyug promise to limit his presence to only 5 places in his kingdom - in gambling dens, in pubs where liquor was served, in places where immoral women lived, in slaughter houses and in gold. During the reign of Parikshit, Kalyug remained true to his word, dwelling in only those places where he had been allowed. It was only later that he started extending his activities to other areas too.

Meanwhile, even Parikshit was not immune to the impact of Kaliyug. He had succeeded in limiting its influence, but did not realize that he had allowed the demon to make his crown its home, since it too was made of gold. This would soon be the cause of his downfall.

One day, Parikshit went hunting in the forest surrounding Hastinapur. Wandering deeper into the forest than usual, he came across an ashram. Hungry and thirsty, he entered the ashram in the hope of getting some food and water, but found only a sage sitting in deep meditation. Tormented by hunger, he tried to wake the sage, but to no avail. Parikshit was tired after a hard day, and was in an upset mood. Moreover, under the influence of Kaliyug, who had been on the lookout for a suitable opportunity to cloud his discrimination, he was overcome by anger and filled with a desire to punish the sage. Looking around, he saw a dead snake on the floor, and with his sword, he put it around the sage's neck and left.

The sage was the great Shameek, who was engaged in deep austerities, and was completely unaware of the events taking place around him. The misconduct of the king came to light only when the sage's son Shringi returned to the ashram and found his father with a dead snake around his neck. He sat down in meditation and was able to see the culprit behind this shameful act. He cursed the king that he would die in seven days, after being bitten by the most venomous of snakes, Takshak himself!

Meanwhile, the sage Shameek awoke from his meditational trance, and regretted the hasty action of his son, which would cause the death of a great and just king. Since the curse could not be retracted, he instructed his son Shringi to at least inform the king of his approaching demise.

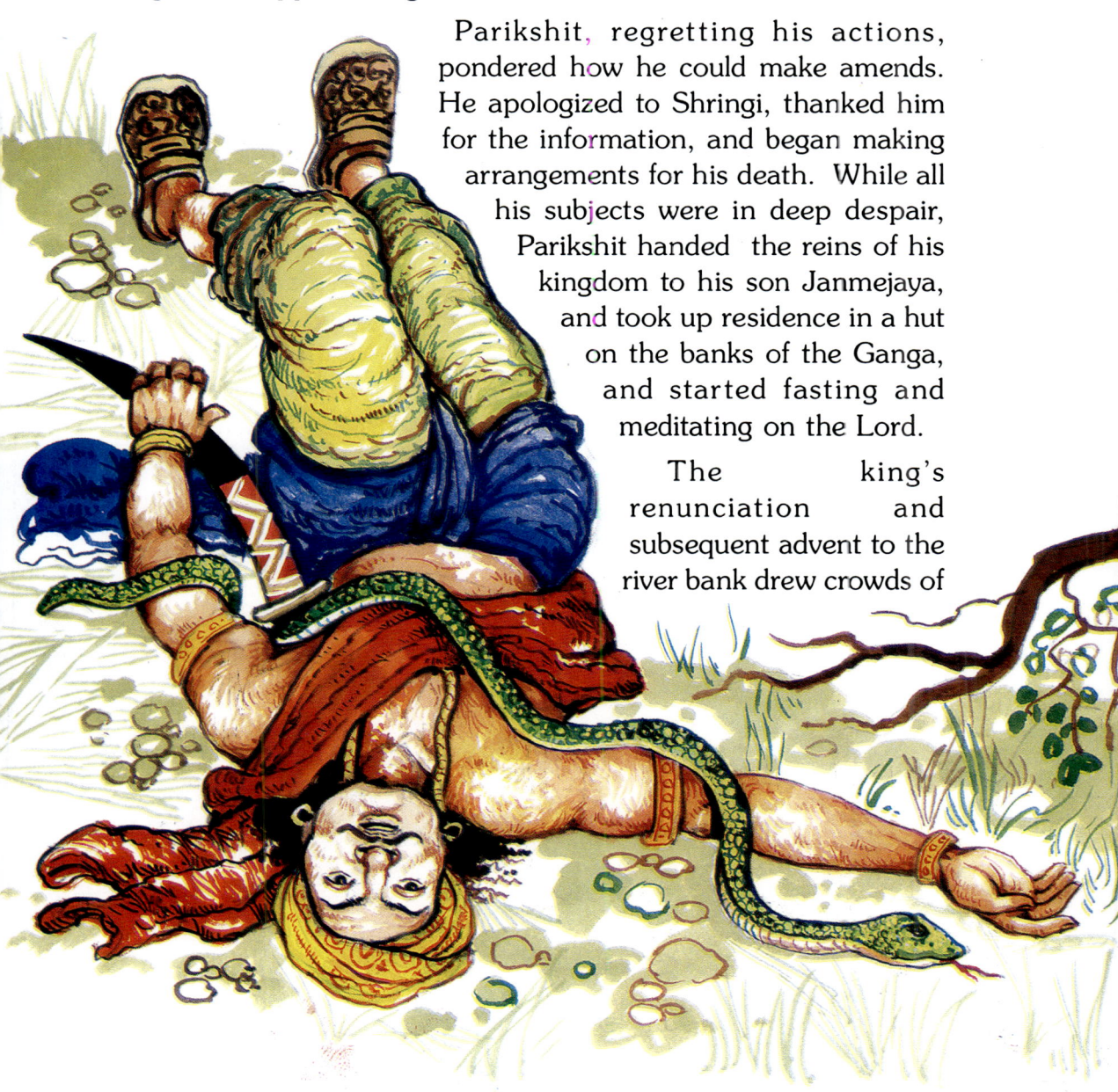

Parikshit, regretting his actions, pondered how he could make amends. He apologized to Shringi, thanked him for the information, and began making arrangements for his death. While all his subjects were in deep despair, Parikshit handed the reins of his kingdom to his son Janmejaya, and took up residence in a hut on the banks of the Ganga, and started fasting and meditating on the Lord.

The king's renunciation and subsequent advent to the river bank drew crowds of sages there, who guessed that a great event was about to happen. Shukadev Paramahans, the son of Ved Vyas also arrived. Parikshit was thrilled to see the young sage, for this was the best opportunity for him to learn the history of his own ancestors and hear about the pastimes of Shree Krishna. Shukadev had heard these *leelas,* or pastimes, from Ved Vyas, his father, the great sage who had written the Mahabharat.

On Parikshit's request, Shukadev Paramahans narrated to the sages present, the story of Lord Shree Krishna, revealing His many forms, teachings and His Divine pastimes. The dialogue that took place between Shukadev Paramahans and Parikshit, is the Shreemad Bhagavatam, one of the most important of Hindu scriptures.

Having related the pastimes and teachigns of the Lord in seven days to Parikshit, Shukadev left, saying, "O King, you have been blessed with the opportunity to engage your last moments to listen to the name of the Lord. By virtue of your lifelong devotion to Shree Krishna, you have already gained your place in His abode. Go and meet your fate with open arms."

When Takshak arrived to bite and kill the king, he found that Parikshit had already left for Golok, the Divine abode of his Lord Krishna. Only the physical body was remaining, that he bit and turned to mud.

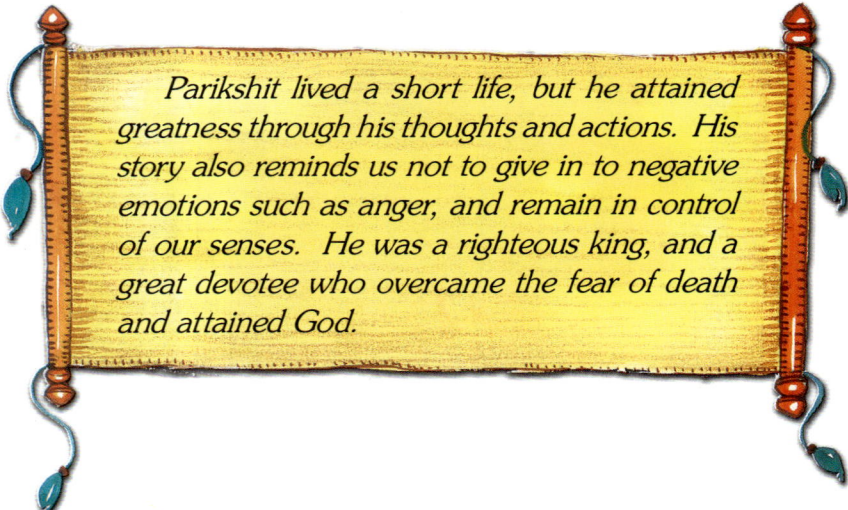

Parikshit lived a short life, but he attained greatness through his thoughts and actions. His story also reminds us not to give in to negative emotions such as anger, and remain in control of our senses. He was a righteous king, and a great devotee who overcame the fear of death and attained God.

Hanuman

Hanuman, one of the greatest devotees of Lord Ram, is famous for his unshakable devotion and absolute dedication towards his Beloved Lord. Amongst all the personalities who participated in the Divine *leelas* of Shree Ram, he is one of the most adored.

He was the son of the wind god Vayu and Anjana, an *apsara,* or celestial maiden, who had been cursed to take the form of a monkey. As a child, he was mischievous and constantly kept the family on their toes with his antics.

One day, he saw the rising sun through the leaves of a mango tree and mistook it to for a luscious mango. He jumped into the air trying to catch it, and with the power of Vayu behind him, soon approached the Sun. Suryadev, the Sun God, was alarmed seeing someone hurtling through the air towards him, and he had to seek the help of Indra, the king of heaven, to stop Hanuman.

As he grew older, Hanuman grew more mischievous, using his special powers to create havoc for people and having fun at their expense. One day, he troubled some sages to such an extent that in rage they cursed him that he would be unable to remember his special powers unless someone reminded him of them.

Forgetting his powers turned Hanuman to more sober deeds, and he was accepted by Suryadev, the Sun God, as his pupil. In response to Suryadev's suggestion, Hanuman befriended Sugreev, a monkey king who had been exiled from his kingdom by his brother Vaali. Hanuman joined Sugreev and his band of monkeys on the Rishyamukha mountain.

In the meantime, Mother Seeta, the wife of Lord Ram, was kidnapped by Ravan and forcibly taken to his kingdom Lanka.

Shree Ram and his brother Lakshman wandered around in the forests in search of her. When they arrived at the Rishyamukha mountain, Sugreev

saw them from afar and sent Hanuman to determine their identity. When Lord Ram introduced himself, Hanuman felt he had found his Lord, and maintained a permanent bond with Him thereafter.

Hanuman took Ram and Lakshman to Sugreev who mentioned that he and other monkeys had seen a beautiful woman being carried away by a demon, but had no idea who she was. They had gathered and kept the pieces of jewelry she had thrown from the skies towards them.

Ram identified Seeta's jewelry, and wept in remembrance of her. In order to rescue Seeta from the demon's clutches and punish the demon, he asked Sugreev's help in locating her.

On Sugreev's request, Lord Ram helped him get his kingdom back from Vaali. He killed Vaali and reinstated Sugreev as the king of the monkeys. In return, Sugreev sent his vast army of monkeys in all directions to search for Seeta.

During the course of their search, the aged and wise bear Jambavan reminded Hanuman of his powers and the curse that had made him forget them. At once, Hanuman was conscious of his great strength, and capability of doing the impossible feats. He willed himself to grow in stature until he stood taller than the highest hills on the seashore, and leaped into the air and flew over the ocean.

Meeting many obstacles on the way, he overcame all of them with strength and intelligence, and finally landed on the island of Lanka. He entered the walled city after overpowering the gatekeeper, and after a long search found Seeta imprisoned in a garden called Ashok Vatika.

He introduced himself to Seeta and proved his identity as a messenger of Lord Ram by showing her a ring he had brought

119

from Him. He volunteered to carry Mother Seeta back to Lord Ram at once, but the virtuous Seeta refused, saying it would not be right. She wanted her husband to be the one to free her from the demon, in addition to releasing other people in captivity.

Finally, he reassured Seeta that her Lord would soon come, defeat Ravan, and avenge her humiliation.

His mission accomplished, Hanuman meditated on a way to reassure Seeta further, and put the fear of Lord Ram into the hearts of the people and the

king of Lanka. He created a disturbance in the gardens, and killed the guards. He incited the army to fight, and then killed many demons, before allowing himself to be caught and taken to the palace, so that he could meet the demon king Ravan.

He warned Ravan to set Seeta free at once, for Lord Ram was on his way to rescue her, but Ravan laughed at the impertinence of a mere monkey, and ordered his tail to be set on fire. With the name of Lord Ram on his lips, Hanuman allowed his tail to be lighted, but the fire did not scorch him. Instead, he set the city of Lanka on fire with it, leaving only the Ashok Vatika unblemished, and set out on his return journey.

The good news spurred Shree Ram's army of monkeys and bears towards the ocean. With exceptional fervor and devotion, a bridge was built of stones, boulders and hills, with the name of Lord Ram inscribed on them. Soon the army crossed the ocean to reached Lanka. Before the war, Ravan was offered peace, provided he set Seeta free, but he refused the offer, and the war began.

Hanuman killed many demons with his great strength. When Lord Ram's brother Lakshman was fatally wounded by Indrajit, the son of Ravan, the physician Sushen announced that the only herb capable of saving Lakshman was the Sanjeevani, which grew on the Dronagiri mountain in the Himalayas. The Himalayas were far, far away, and the herb had to be brought back before sunrise for it to work. How would it be possible?

Nothing was impossible for Hanuman, and he set out for the Himalayas, taking an immense form, and flying through the air. Ravan learned of his intention and sent his uncle, the dreaded Kalanemi to stop him, but Hanuman killed Kalanemi and reached the mountain. He encountered a problem he had not anticipated. The mountain was covered with herbs, and he was unable to identify

the right one. There was no time to lose, so he simply lifted the whole mountain and flew back to Lanka.

The monkeys were stunned at the sight of Hanuman carrying the mountain, but they set to work, collecting the right herbs and reviving not just Lakshman, but all the monkeys who had been wounded. After the war was over, Hanuman made the journey again and replaced the mountain in its original place.

Hanuman showed his prowess again when Ravan's half-brothers Ahi Ravan and Mahi Ravan captured Shree Ram and Lakshman and took them to Patal, the hellish realm. It was Hanuman, who bravely entered the nether region, and rescued them, after killing the demons.

Hanuman was the greatest devotee of Lord Ram, and after the period of exile ended, he was the one who went to Ayodhya and informed Bharat of Lord Ram's return.

Lord Ram's coronation was a great and much anticipated event, which was attended by the entire army that had helped Lord Ram. After the coronation was over, Ram and Seeta bestowed expensive gifts upon everyone. For Hanuman, Seeta took off one of her own pearl necklace and handed it to him. Everyone was surprised when Hanuman did not show much enthusiasm over the gift, but instead, scrutinized each pearl and appeared dissatisfied.

Finally, Seeta asked him if he was unhappy with the gift, to which Hanuman replied, "Of what use is something which does not have Lord Ram in it?" This answer astonished everyone, and finally someone asked jokingly, "If that is so, is Lord Ram inside you too?" Hanuman did not utter a word, but simply tore his chest open. And lo behold! There were Lord Ram and Mother Seeta seated in his heart. Such was the devotion and love of Hanuman towards Lord Ram.

When Lord Ram decided to go back to His abode, he asked those who wanted to join him, to come along. While most of the monkeys and his citizens elected to accompany Lord Ram, Hanuman had a unique request – he wanted to remain on the earth as long as the people venerated Shree Ram's name. Lord Ram granted Hanuman the boon, so that in future, he could be present wherever the name of Ram was taken with love and reverence.

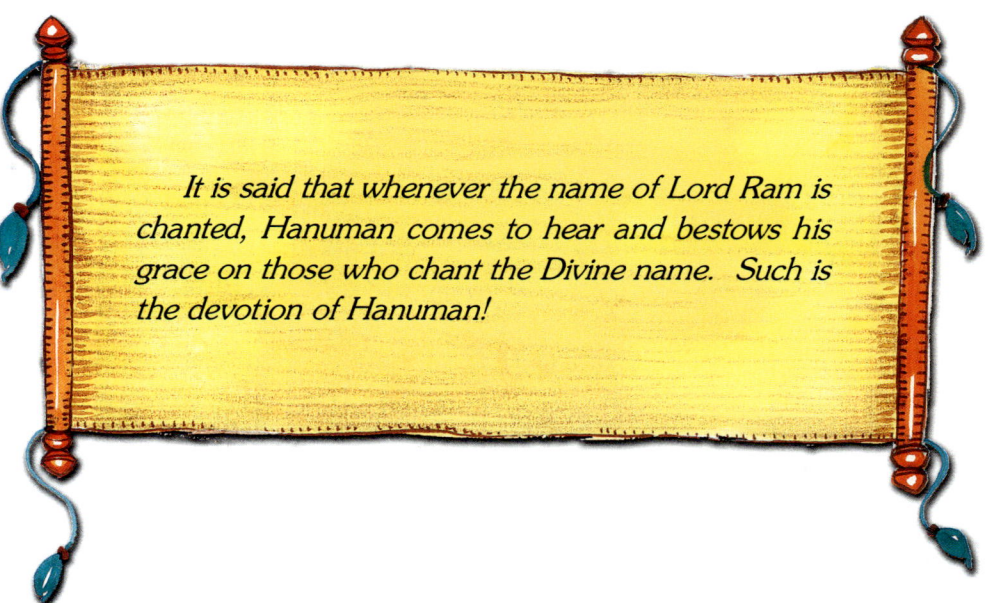

It is said that whenever the name of Lord Ram is chanted, Hanuman comes to hear and bestows his grace on those who chant the Divine name. Such is the devotion of Hanuman!

Vidur

Vidur was one of the wisest personalities who lived in the time of Shree Krishna. Born of a maidservant of Ambika and Ambalika, the wives of Vichitravirya, Vidur was the half brother of Pandu and Dhritarashtra.

Though he had two wives, Vichitravirya was unable to beget children, and the great sage Ved Vyas was summoned for consultation. Faced with the powerful aura of the sage, Ambika shut her eyes while Ambalika turned pale and weak. Only the maidservant accompanying them remained calm, and in due course, children were born to all three of them. While Ambika's son was born blind, Ambalika's son was frail and weak. It was the maid's son who was born with the knowledge and wisdom of the great sage, and grew to be Vidur – respected by the young and old alike.

Vidur was an incarnation of Yamraj, or Dharmaraj, the god of righteousness and also of death. Yamraj incarnated as Vidur due to the curse of the sage Mandavya. The sage had acquired great strength of mind and knowledge of the scriptures, and spent his time in penance, living in his ashram on the outskirts of the city. Once, a band of thieves who had robbed the palace came that way, followed by the king's guards. Seeing the ashram, they hid the loot in a corner and ran away. The king's guards entered the ashram and asked the sage about the robbers, but he was so deep in meditation that he was not aware of the happenings around him. Meanwhile, the guards discovered the loot in the cottage and concluded that the sage was one of the robbers disguised. They impaled the sage with a spear and returned to the city.

Meanwhile, the other sages in the area came to know of the incident and arrived at the ashram, and the king, getting the news, arrived too, afraid of the sage's reaction. However, the sage, when he came to himself, was far from angry with the king or his guards. He wondered which of his past misdeeds would have earned him such torture, and accordingly went to Yamraj with the question.

Yamraj answered, "O sage, it is indeed your past deeds which earned you this punishment. As a child, you tortured insects and other small creatures, which is why you suffered the same fate as them." Hearing this, the sage was angry and said, "The punishment you have decreed for the act of an innocent child is far too harsh. Be born, therefore as a mortal on earth." It was in response to this curse that Yamraj incarnated as Vidur, and epitomized the ideal of knowledge without attachment, ego or anger.

As the son of a maidservant, Vidur was never considered a contender for the throne of Hastinapur. However, Bheesma insisted on educating him on par with his brothers and made him their minister. Even at an early age, Vidur displayed his greatness and wisdom, guiding his royal half-brothers on the right way to rule the kingdom.

Vidur, as the chief counsel to Dhritarashtra, continually advised him against wrongdoing, even when he knew that his counsel would go unheeded. Once, Dhritarashtra was so angry at his advice that he ordered him to leave the city at once. Vidur, without an angry word in response, left the city and headed towards the abode of the Pandavas. However, Dhritarashtra soon realized his error and sent messengers to bring back Vidur, who agreed and came back. He did not harbor any negative feelings towards Dhritarasthra, for was firm in simply doing his duty, and did not care if people glorified or misbehaved with him.

Vidur was also among the few people who were aware of the Divinity of Lord Krishna. When Shree Krishna arrived at Hastinapur to advise Duryodhan against the war, He chose to stay at Vidur's humble dwelling, instead of the grand palace designated for Him. Vidur and his wife were thrilled and made every arrangement possible for their Divine guest.

An interesting story illustrates the love that Vidur's wife had for Shree Krishna. On coming to know that Shree Krishna would be coming to his house, Vidur rushed to the market to purchase foodstuffs for his Divine guest. However, Shree Krishna reached before Vidur could return, and began knocking on the door. When Vidurani opened the door and saw her Beloved Lord at her doorstep, she was overcome with happiness, and catching His hand, brought Him in.

Desiring to feed Shree Krishna with her own hands, she went to the kitchen and brought a bunch of bananas. However, she was so deeply absorbed in devotional thoughts that she began dropping the fruit and putting the banana peel in Shree Krishna's mouth. Krishna calmly ate the peels without uttering a word. This blunder was discovered only when Vidur reached home and saw what his wife was doing. He scolded Vidurani, and offered the food items he had brought to Shree Krishna. The Lord savored

them, but remarked that they did not taste as sweet as the banana peels of Vidurani, because they had been offered with such love. Through this pastime, Shree Krishna revealed that the Lord would accept anything offered with devotion, not just the fruits, but the peels too!

Once the Mahabharat war was over, Vidur continued to counsel the Pandavas in the righteous way of governance. When the time came, it was he who made Dhritarashtra and Gandhari aware that it was time for them to leave for the forest, giving up their attachment to worldly life. Kunti elected to go with them too, and all four of them entered the forest together. While Kunti, Dhritarashtra and Gandhari soon left their bodies and attained heaven, Vidur continued his penance until the time came for him to leave his mortal body.

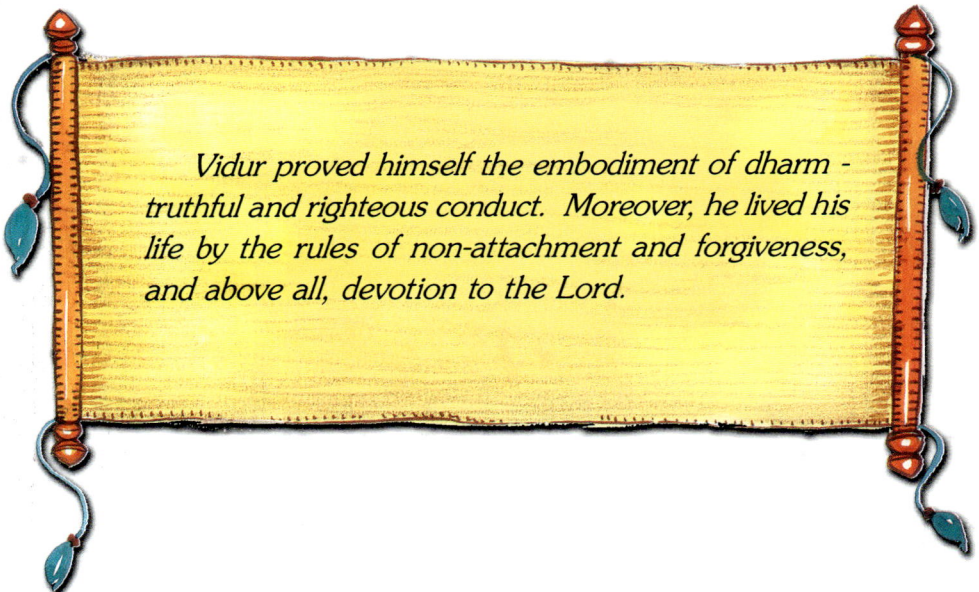

Vidur proved himself the embodiment of dharm - truthful and righteous conduct. Moreover, he lived his life by the rules of non-attachment and forgiveness, and above all, devotion to the Lord.

BAL-MUKUND CHARACTER BUILDING SERIES

1. Inspiring Stories for Children, Vol 1

2. Inspiring Stories for Children, Vol 2

3. Inspiring Stories for Children, Vol 3

4. Inspiring Stories for Children, Vol 4

5. Festivals of India

6. Saints of India

7. The Bal-Mukund WISDOM Book

8. The Bal-Mukund Painting Book

Audio CDs

1. The Bal-Mukund WISDOM Book-Prayers and Keertans

2. The Bal-Mukund WISDOM Book-Shlokas & Verses

3. Bal-Mukund Meditation for Children